THE GOSPEL OF JOHN

William Kelly

The Works of William Kelly are works of Public Domain.

Unless otherwise indicated, the biblical quotations contained in this book are taken from the King James Version First Edition 1611 (Public Domain) edited and updated by the editors according to the best of contemporary conservative textual criticism.

Collected Works of William Kelly

CONTENTS

PREFACE 3

JOHN 1-7 4

JOHN 8-14 43

JOHN 15-21 86

PREFACE

The volume before the reader pretends to be nothing more than a rapid sketch of the four inspired accounts of our blessed Lord, which the Holy Ghost has been pleased to give for our instruction and joy through the faith of Him who is there revealed to us. Eleven discourses delivered in London (between May 31st and June 20th, 1866) did not afford much space for details. Taken in shorthand, they were corrected by the lecturer, with additions and retrenchments. He now commits the book, spite of shortcoming abundant, to His blessing who loved the Church and gave Himself for it, who still nourishes and cherishes it with tender care. May He graciously pardon every thought, feeling, and word inconsistent with Himself! May He deign to own and use the thing spoken of Him that is right!

William Kelly
Guernsey, 18th December 1866.

JOHN 1-7

The opening verses (John 1:1-18) introduce the most glorious subject which God Himself ever gave in employing the pen of man; not only the most glorious in point of theme, but in the profoundest point of view; for what the Holy Ghost here brings before us is the Word, the everlasting, Word, when He was with God, traced down from before all time, when there was no creature. It is not exactly the Word with the Father; for such a phrase would not be according to the exactness of the truth; but the Word with God. The term God comprehends not only the Father, but the Holy Ghost also. He who was the Son of the Father then, as I need not say always, is regarded here as the revealer of God; for God, as such, does not reveal Himself. He makes His, nature known by the Word. The Word, nevertheless, is here spoken of before there was any one for God to reveal Himself to. He is, therefore, and in the strictest sense, eternal. "In the beginning was the Word," when there was no reckoning of time; for the beginning of what we call time comes before us in the third verse. "All things," it is said, "were made by Him." This is clearly the origination of all creature hood, wherever and whatever it be. Heavenly beings there were before the earthly; but whether — no matter of whom you speak, or of, what — angels or men, whether heaven or earth, all things were made by Him.

Thus He, whom we know to be the Son of the Father, is here presented as the Word — who subsisted personally in the beginning (ἐν ἀρχῇ) — who was with God, and was Himself God — of the same nature, yet a distinct personal being. To clench this matter specially against all reveries of Gnostics or others, it is added, that He was in the beginning with God[1]. Observe

---

[1] I cannot but regard John 1:2 as a striking and complete setting aside of the Alexandrian and Patristic distinction of λόγος ἐνδιάθετος and λόγος προφορικός. Some of the earlier Greek fathers, who were infected with Platonism, held that the λόγος was conceived in God's mind from eternity,

another thing: "The Word was with God" — not the Father. As the Word and God, so the Son and the Father are correlative. We are here in the exactest phrase, and at the same time in the briefest terms, brought into the presence of the deepest conceivable truths which God, alone knowing, alone could communicate to man. Indeed, it is He alone who gives the truth; for this is not the bare knowledge of such or such facts, whatever the accuracy of the information. Were all things conveyed with the most admirable correctness, it would not amount to divine revelation. Such a communication would still differ, not in degree only, but in kind. A revelation from God not only supposes true statements, but God's mind made known so as to act morally on man, forming his thoughts and affections according to His own character. God makes Himself known in what He communicates by, of, and in Christ.

In the case before us, nothing can be more obvious than that the Holy Ghost, for the glory of God, is undertaking to make known that which touches the Godhead in the closest way, and is meant for infinite blessing to all in the person of the Lord Jesus. These verses accordingly begin with Christ our Lord; not from, but in the beginning, when nothing was yet created. It is the eternity of His being, in no point of which could it be said He was not, but, contrariwise, that He was. Yet was He not alone. God was there — not the Father only, but the Holy Ghost, beside the Word Himself, who was God, and had divine nature as they.

Again, it is not said that in the beginning He was, in the sense of then coming into being (ἐγένετο), but He existed (ἦν). Thus before all time the Word was. When the great truth of the incarnation is noted in verse 14, it is said — not that the Word came into existence, but that He was made (ἐγένετο) flesh —

---

and only uttered, as it were, in time. This has given a handle to Arians, who, like other unbelievers, greedily seek the traditions of men. The apostle here asserts, in the Holy Ghost, the eternal personality of the Word with God.

began so to be. This, therefore, so much the more contrasts with verses 1 and 2.

In the beginning, then, before there was any creature, was the Word, and the Word was with God. There was distinct personality in the Godhead, therefore, and the Word was a distinct person Himself (not, as men dreamt, an emanation in time, though eternal and divine in nature, proceeding from God as its source). The Word had a proper personality, and at the same time was God — "the Word was God." Yea, as the next verse binds and sums up all together, He, the Word, was in the beginning with God. The personality was as eternal as the existence, not in (after some mystic sort) but with God. I can conceive no statement more admirably complete and luminous in the fewest and simplest words.

Next comes the attributing of creation to the Word. This must be the work of God, if anything was; and here again the words are precision itself — "All things were made by him, and without him was not anything made that was made." Other words far less nervous are used elsewhere: unbelief might cavil and construe them into forming or fashioning. Here the Holy Ghost employs the most explicit language, that all things began to be, or received being, through the Word, to the exclusion of one single thing that ever did receive being apart from Him language which leaves the fullest room for Uncreate Beings, as we have already seen, subsisting eternally and distinctly, yet equally God. Thus the statement is positive that the Word is the source of all things which have received being (γενόμενα); that there is no creature which did not thus derive its being from Him. There cannot, therefore, be a more rigid, absolute shutting out of any creature from origination, save by the Word.

It is true that in other parts of Scripture we hear God, as such, spoken of as Creator. We hear of His making the worlds by the Son. But there is and can be no contradiction in Scripture. The truth is, that whatever was made was made according to the

Father's sovereign will; but the Son, the Word of God, was the person who put forth the power, and never without the energy of the Holy Ghost, I may add, as the Bible carefully teaches us. Now this is of immense importance for that which the Holy Ghost has in view in the gospel of John, because the object is to attest the nature and light of God in the person of the Christ; and therefore we have here not merely what the Lord Jesus was as born of a woman, born under the law, which has its appropriate place in the gospels of Matthew and Luke, but what He was and is as God. On the other hand, the gospel of Mark omits everything of the kind. A genealogy such as Matthew's and Luke's, we have seen, would be totally out of place there; and the reason is manifest. The subject of Mark is the testimony of Jesus as having taken, though a Son, the place of a servant in the earth. Now, in a servant, no matter from what noble lineage he comes, there is no genealogy requisite. What is wanted in a servant is, that the work should be done well, no matter about the genealogy. Thus, even if it were the Son of God Himself, so perfectly did He condescend to the condition of a servant, and so mindful was the Spirit of it, that, accordingly, the genealogy which was demanded in Matthew, which is of such signal beauty and value in Luke, is necessarily excluded from the gospel of Mark. For higher reasons it could have no place in John. In Mark it is because of the lowly place of subjection which the Lord was pleased to take; it is excluded from John, on the contrary, because there He is presented as being above all genealogy . He is the source of other people's genealogy — yea, of the genesis of all things. We may say therefore boldly, that in the gospel of John such a descent could not be inserted in consistency with its character. If it admit any genealogy, it must be what is set forth in the preface of John — the very verses which are occupying us — which exhibit the divine nature and eternal personality of His being. He was the Word, and He was God; and, if we may anticipate, let us add, the Son, the only begotten Son of the Father. This, if anything, is His genealogy here. The ground is evident; because everywhere in John He is God. No doubt the Word became flesh, as we may see more of presently, even in this inspired introduction; and we have the reality of His becoming man insisted on. Still, manhood was a place that He entered. Godhead was the glory that He possessed from everlasting — His own eternal nature of being. It was not conferred upon Him. There is not, nor can be, any such thing as a derived subordinate Godhead; though men may be said to be gods, as commissioned of God, and representing Him in government. He was God before creation began, before all time. He was God independently of any circumstances. Thus, as we have seen, for the Word the apostle John claims eternal existence, distinct personality, and divine nature; and withal asserts the eternal distinctness of that person. (Verses 1, 2)

Such is the Word Godward (πρὸς τὸν Θεόν). We are next told of Him in relation to the creature. (Verses 3-5) In the earlier verses it was exclusively His being. In verse 3 He acts, He creates, He causes all things to come into existence; and apart from Him not one thing came into existence which is existent (γέγονεν). Nothing more comprehensive, nothing more exclusive.

The next verse (4) predicts of Him that which is yet more momentous: not creative power, as in verse 3, but life. "In him was life." Blessed truth for those who know the spread of death over this lower scene of creation! and the rather as the Spirit adds, that "the life was the light of men." Angels were not its sphere, nor was it restricted to a chosen nation: "the life was the light of men." Life was not in man, even unfallen; at best, the first man, Adam, became a living soul when instinct with the breath of God. Nor is it ever said, even of a saint, that in him is or was life, though life he has; but he has it only in the Son. In Him, the Word, was life, and the life was the light of men. Such was its relationship.

No doubt, whatever was revealed of old was of Him; whatever word came out from God was from Him, the Word, and light of men. But then God was not revealed; for He was not manifested. On the contrary, He dwelt in the thick darkness, behind the veil in the most holy place, or visiting men but angelically otherwise. But here, we are told, "the light shines in the darkness." (Ver. 5) Mark the abstractedness of the language — it "shines" (not shone). How solemn, that darkness is all the light finds! and what darkness! how impenetrable and hopeless! All other darkness yields and fades away before light; but here "the darkness comprehended it not" (as the fact is stated, and not the abstract principle only). It was suited to man, even as it was the light expressly of men, so that man is without excuse.

But was there adequate care that the light should be presented to men? What was the way taken to secure this? Unable God could not be: was He indifferent? God gave testimony; first, John the Baptist; then the Light itself. "There was (ἐγένετο) a man sent from God, whose name was John." (v. 6) He passes by all the prophets, the various preliminary dealings of the Lord, the shadows of the law: not even the promises are noticed here. We shall find some of these introduced or alluded to for a far different purpose later on. John, then, came to bear witness about the Light, that all through him might believe. (Verse 7) But the Holy Ghost is most careful to guard against all mistake. Could any run too close a parallel between the light of men in the Word, and him who is called the burning and shining lamp in a subsequent chapter? Let them learn their error. He, John, "was not that light;" there is but one such: none was similar or second. God cannot be compared with man. John came "that he might bear witness about the light," not to take its place or set himself up. The true Light was that which, coming into the world, lighteth every man[2]. Not only does He necessarily, as being God, deal with every man (for His glory could not be restricted to a part of mankind), but the weighty truth here announced is the

---

[2] I cannot but think that this is the true version, and exhibits the intended aim of the clause. Most of the early writers took it as the authorized version, save Theodore of Mopsuestia, who understood it as here given: Εἰπὼν τὸ· ἐρχόμενον εἰς τὸν κοσμον, περὶ τοῦ δεσπότου Χριστοῦ καλῶς ἐπήγαγεν τὸ· ἐν τῳ κοσμῳ ἦν, ὥστε δεῖξαι, ὅτι τὸ ἐρχόμενον πρὸς τὴν διὰ σαρκὸς εἶπεν φανέρωσιν (Ed. Fritzsche, p. 21).

connection with His incarnation of this universal light, or revelation of God in Him, to man as such. The law, as we know from elsewhere, had dealt with the Jewish people temporarily, and for partial purposes. This was but a limited sphere. Now that the Word comes into the world, in one way or another light shines for everyone: it may be, leaving some under condemnation, as we know it does for the great mass who believe not; it may be light not only on but in man, where there is faith through the action of divine grace. It is certain that, whatever light in relation to God there may be, and wherever it is given in Him, there is not, there never was, spiritual light apart from Christ — all else is darkness. It could not be otherwise. This light in its own character must go out to all from God. So it is said elsewhere, "The grace of God that bringeth salvation to all men hath appeared." It is not that all men receive the blessing; but, in its proper scope and nature, it addresses itself to all. God sends it for all. Law may govern one nation; grace refuses to be limited in its appeal, however it may be in fact through man's unbelief.

"He was in the world, and the world was made by him." (Verse 9) The world therefore surely ought to have known its Maker. Nay, "the world knew him not." From the very first, man, being a sinner, was wholly lost. Here the unlimited scene is in view; not Israel, but the world. Nevertheless, Christ did come to His own things, His proper, peculiar possession; for there were special relationships. They should have understood more about Him — those that were specially favoured. It was not so.

"He came unto his own [things], and his own [people] received him not. But as many as received him, to them gave the power [rather, authority, right, or title] to become children of God." (Ver. 11, 12) It was not a question now of Jehovah and His servants. Neither does the Spirit say exactly as the English Bible says — "sons," but children. His glorious person would have none now in relation to God but members of the family. Such was the grace that God was displaying in Him, the true and full expresser of His mind. He gave them title to take the place of children of God, even to those that believe on His name. Sons they might have been in bare title; but these had the right of children.

All disciplinary action, every probationary process, disappears. The ignorance of the world has been proved, the rejection of Israel is complete: then only is it that we hear of this new place of children. It is now eternal reality, and the name of Jesus Christ is that which puts all things to a final test. There is difference of manner for the world and His own — ignorance and rejection. Do any believe on His name? Be they who they may now, as many as receive Him become children of God. It is no question here of every man, but of such as believe. Do they receive Him not? For them, Israel, or the world, all is over. Flesh and world are judged morally. God the Father forms a new family in, by, and for Christ. All others prove not only that they are bad, but that they hate perfect goodness, and more than that, life and light — the true light in the Word. How can such have relationship with God?

Thus, manifestly, the whole question is terminated at the very starting-point of our gospel; and this is characteristic of John all through: manifestly all is decided. It is not merely a Messiah, who comes and offers Himself, as we find in other gospels, with most painstaking diligence, and presented to their responsibility; but here from the outset the question is viewed as closed. The Light, on coming into the world, lightens every man with the fulness of evidence which was in Him, and at once discovers the true state as truly as it will be revealed in the last day when He judges all, as we find it intimated in the gospel afterwards. (John 12:48)

Before the manner of His manifestation comes before us in verse 14, we have the secret explained why some, and not all, received Christ. It was not that they were better than their neighbours. Natural birth had nothing to do with this new thing; it was a new nature altogether in those who received Him: "Who were born, not of blood, nor of the will of the flesh, nor of the will of man, but of God." It was an extraordinary birth; of God, not man in any sort, or measure, but a new and divine nature (2 Peter 1) imparted to the believer wholly of grace. All this, however, was abstract, whether as to the nature of the Word or as to the place of the Christian.

But it is important we should know how He entered the world. We have seen already that thus light was shed on men. How was this? The Word, in order to accomplish these infinite things, "was made. (ἐγένετο) flesh, and dwelt among us." It is here we learn in what condition of His person God was to be revealed and the work done; not what He was in nature, but what He became. The great fact of the incarnation is brought before us — "The Word was made flesh, and dwelt among us (and we beheld his glory, the glory as of the only-begotten of the Father"). His aspect as thus tabernacling among the disciples was "full of grace and truth." Observe, that blessed as the light is, being God's moral nature, truth is more than this, and is introduced by grace. It is the revelation of God — yea, of the Father and the Son, and not merely the detecter of man. The Son had not come to execute the judgments of the law they knew, nor even to promulgate a new and higher law. His was an errand incomparably deeper, more worthy of God, and suitable to One "full of grace and truth." He wanted nothing; He came to give — yea, the very best, so to speak, that God has.

What is there in God more truly divine than grace and truth? The incarnate Word was here full of grace and truth. Glory would be displayed in its day. Meanwhile there was a manifestation of goodness, active in love in the midst of evil, and toward such; active in the making known God and man, and every moral relation, and what He is toward man, through and in the Word made flesh. This is grace and truth. And such was Jesus. "John bare witness of him, and cried, saying, This is he of whom I spake: He that cometh after me is preferred before me, for he was before me." Coming after John as to date, He is necessarily preferred before him in dignity; for He was (ἦν) [not come into being (ἐγένετο)] before Him. He was God. This statement (verse 15) is a parenthesis, though confirmatory of verse 14, and connects John's testimony with this new section of Christ's manifestation in flesh; as we saw John introduced in the earlier verses, which treated abstractly of Christ's nature as the Word.

Then, resuming the strain of verse 14, we are told, in verse 16, that "of his fulness have all we received." So rich and transparently divine was the grace: not some souls, more meritorious than the rest, rewarded according to a graduated scale of honour, but "of his fulness have all we received." What can be conceived more notably standing out in contrast with the governmental system God had set up, and man had known in times past? Here there could not be more, and He would not give less: even "grace upon grace." Spite of the most express signs, and the manifest finger of God that wrote the ten words on tables of stone, the law sinks into comparative insignificance. "The law was given by Moses." God does not here condescend to call it His, though, of course, it was His — and holy, just, and good, both in itself and in its use, if used lawfully. But if the Spirit speaks of the Son of God, the law dwindles at once into the smallest possible proportions: everything yields to the honour the Father puts oil the Son. "The law was given by Moses, but grace and truth came (ἐγένετο) by Jesus Christ." (ver. 17) The law, thus given, was in itself no giver, but an exacter; Jesus, full of grace and truth, gave, instead of requiring or receiving; and He Himself has said, It is more blessed to give than to receive. Truth and grace were not sought nor found in man, but began to subsist here below by Jesus Christ.

We have now the Word made flesh, called Jesus Christ — this person, this complex person, that was manifest in the world; and it is He that brought it all in. Grace and truth came by Jesus Christ.

Lastly, closing this part, we have another most remarkable contrast. "No man hath seen God at any time: the only-begotten Son," etc. Now, it is no longer a question of nature, but of relationship; and hence it is not said simply the Word, but the Son, and the Son in the highest possible character, the only-begotten Son, distinguishing Him thus from any other who might, in a subordinate sense, be son of God — "the only-begotten Son, which is in the bosom of the Father." Observe: not which was, but "which is." He is viewed as retaining the same perfect intimacy with the Father, entirely unimpaired by local or any other circumstances He had entered. Nothing in the slightest degree detracted from His own personal glory, and from the infinitely near relationship which He had had with the Father from all eternity. He entered this world, became flesh, as born of woman; but there was no diminution of His own glory, when He, born of the virgin, walked on earth, or when rejected of man, cut off as Messiah, He was forsaken of God for sin — our sin — on the cross. Under all changes, outwardly, He abode as from eternity the only-begotten Son in the bosom of the Father. Mark what, as such, He does declare Him. No man hath seen God at any time. He could be declared only by One who was a divine person in the intimacy of the Godhead, yea, was the only-begotten Son in the bosom of the Father. Hence the Son, being in this ineffable nearness of love, has declared not God only, but the Father. Thus we all not only receive of His fulness, (and what fulness illimitable was there not in Him!) but He, who is the Word made flesh, is the only-begotten Son who is in the bosom of the Father, and so competent to declare, as in fact He has. It is not only the nature, but the model and fulness of the blessing in the Son, who declared the Father.

The distinctiveness of such a testimony to the Saviour's glory need hardly be pointed out. One needs no more than to read, as believers, these wonderful expressions of the Holy Ghost, where we cannot but feel that we are on ground wholly different from that of the other gospels. Of course they are just as truly inspired as John's; but for that very reason they were not inspired to give the same testimony. Each had his own; all are harmonious, all perfect, all divine; but not all so many repetitions of the same thing. He who inspired them to communicate His thoughts of Jesus in the particular line assigned to each, raised up John to impart the highest revelation, and thus complete the circle by the deepest views of the Son of God.

After this we have, suitably to this gospel, John's connection with the Lord Jesus. (ver. 19-37) It is here presented historically. We have had his name introduced into each part of the preface of our evangelist. Here there is no John proclaiming Jesus as the One who was about to introduce the kingdom of heaven. Of this we learn nothing, here. Nothing is said about the fan in His hand; nothing of His burning up the chaff with unquenchable fire. This is all perfectly true, of course; and we have it elsewhere. His earthly rights are just where they should be; but not here, where the only-begotten Son who is in the bosom of the Father has His appropriate place. It is not John's business here to call attention to His Messiahship, not even when the Jews sent priests and Levites from Jerusalem to ask, Who art thou? Nor was it from any indistinctness in the record, or in him who gave it. For "he confessed, and denied not; but confessed, I am not the Christ. And they asked him, What then? Art thou Elias? And he saith, I am not. Art thou that prophet? And he answered, No. Then said they unto him, who art thou? that we may give an answer to them that sent us. What sayest thou of thyself? He said, I am the voice of one crying in the wilderness, make straight the way of the Lord, as said the prophet Esaias. And they which were sent were of the Pharisees. And they asked him, and said unto him, why baptizest thou then, if thou be not that Christ, nor Elias, neither that prophet? (ver. 20-25) John does not even speak of Him as one who, on His rejection as Messiah, would step into a larger glory. To the Pharisees, indeed, his words as to the Lord are curt: nor does he tell them of the divine ground of His glory, as he had before and does after[3]. He says, One was among them of whom they had no conscious knowledge, "that cometh after me, the thong of whose sandal I am not worthy to loose." (Ver. 26, 27) For himself he was not the Christ, but for Jesus he says no more. How striking the omission! for he knew He was the Christ. But here it was not God's purpose to record it.

Verse 29 opens John's testimony to his disciples. (Ver. 29-34) How rich it is, and how marvellously in keeping with our gospel! Jesus is the Lamb of God that takes away the sin of the world, but withal, as he had said, the eternal One, yet in view of His manifestation to Israel (and, therefore, John was come baptizing with water — a reason here given, but not to the Pharisees in verses 25-27). Further, John attests that he saw the Spirit descending like a dove, and abiding on Him — the appointed token that He it is who baptizes with the Holy Ghost — even the Son of God. None else could do either work: for here we see His great work on earth, and His heavenly power. In these two points of view, more particularly, John gives testimony to Christ; He is the lamb as the taker away of the world's sin; the same is He who baptizeth with the Holy Ghost. Both of them were in relation to man on the earth; the one while He was here, the other from above. His death on the cross included much more, clearly answering to the first; His baptizing with the Holy Ghost followed His going to heaven. Nevertheless, the heavenly part is little dwelt on, as John's gospel displays our Lord more as the expression of God revealed on earth, than as Man ascended to heaven, which fell far more to the province of the apostle of the Gentiles. In John He is One who could be described as Son of man who is in heaven; but He belonged to heaven, because He was divine. His exaltation there is not without notice in the gospel, but exceptionally.

---

[3] The best text omits other expressions, evidently derived from verses 15, 30.

Remark, too, the extent of the work involved in verse 29. As the Lamb of God (of the Father it is not said), He has to do with the world. Nor will the full force of this expression be witnessed till the glorious result of His blood — shedding sweep away the last trace of sin in the new heavens and the new earth, wherein dwelleth righteousness. It finds, of course, a present application, and links itself with that activity of grace in which God is now sending out the gospel to any sinner and every sinner. Still the eternal day alone will show out the full virtue of that which belongs to Jesus as the Lamb of God, who takes away the world's sin. Observe, it is not (as is often very erroneously said or sung) a question of sins, but of the "sin" of the world. The sacrificial death of Him who is God goes far beyond the thought of Israel. How, indeed, could it be stayed within narrow limits? It passes over all question of dispensations, until it accomplishes, in all its extent, that purpose for which He thus died. No doubt there are intervening applications; but such is the ultimate result of His work as the Lamb of God. Even now faith knows, that instead of sin being the great object before God, ever since the cross He has had before His eyes that sacrifice which put away sin. Notably He is now applying it to the reconciliation of a people, who are also baptized by the Holy Ghost into one body. By and by He will apply it to "that nation," the Jews, as to others also, and finally (always excepting the unbelieving and evil) to the entire system, the world. I do not mean by this all individuals, but creation; for nothing can be more certain, than that those who do not receive the Son of God are so much the worse for having heard the gospel. The rejection of Christ is the contempt of God Himself, in that of which He is most jealous, the honour of the Saviour, His Son. The refusal of His precious blood will, on the contrary, make their case incomparably worse than that of the heathen who never heard the good news.

What a witness all this to His person! None but a divine being could thus deal with the world. No doubt He must become a man, in order, amongst other reasons, to be a sufferer, and to die. None the less did the result of His death proclaim His Deity.

So in the baptism with the Holy Ghost, who would pretend to such a power? No mere man, nor angel, not the highest, the archangel, but the Son.

So we see in the attractive power, afterwards dealing with individual souls. For were it not God Himself in the person of Jesus, it had been no glory to God, but a wrong and a rival. For nothing can be more observable than the way in which He becomes the centre round whom those that belong to God are gathered. This is the marked effect on the third day (ver. 29, 34) of John Baptist's testimony here named; the first day (ver. 29) on which, as it were, Jesus speaks and acts in His grace as here shown on the earth. It is evident, that were He not God, it would be an interference with His glory, a place taken inconsistent with His sole authority, no less than it must be also, and for that reason, altogether ruinous to man. But He, being God, was manifesting and, on the contrary, maintaining the divine glory here below. John, therefore, who had been the honoured witness before of God's call, "the voice," etc., does now by the outpouring of his heart's delight, as well as testimony, turn over, so to say, his disciples to Jesus. Beholding Him as He walked, he says, Behold the Lamb of God! and the two disciples leave John for Jesus. (ver. 35-40) Our Lord acts as One fully conscious of His glory, as indeed He ever was.

Bear in mind that one of the points of instruction in this first part of our gospel is the action of the Son of God before His regular Galilean ministry. The first four chapters of John precede in point of time the notices of His ministry in the other gospels. John was not yet cast into prison. Matthew, Mark, and Luke start, as far as regards the public labours of the Lord, with John cast into prison. But all that is historically related of the Lord Jesus in John 1-4. was before the imprisonment of the Baptist. Here, then, we have a remarkable display of that which preceded His Galilean ministry, or public manifestation. Yet before a miracle, as well as in the working of those which set forth His glory, it is evident that so far from its being a gradual growth, as it were, in

His mind, He had, all simple and lowly though He were, the deep, calm, constant consciousness that He was God. He acts as such. If He put forth His power, it was not only beyond man's measure, but unequivocally divine, however also the humblest and most dependent of men. Here we see Him accepting, not as fellow-servant, but as Lord, those souls who had been under the training of the predicted messenger of Jehovah that was to prepare His way before, His face. Also one of the two thus drawn to Him first finds his own brother Simon (with the words, We have found the Messiah), and led him to Jesus, who forthwith gave him his new name in terms which surveyed, with equal ease and certainty, past, present, and future. Here again, apart from this divine insight, the change or gift of the name marks His glory. (Verses 41-44)

On the morrow Jesus begins, directly and indirectly, to call others to follow Himself. He tells Philip to follow Him. This leads Philip to Nathanael, in whose case, when he comes to Jesus, we see not divine power alone in sounding the souls of men, but over creation. Here was One on earth who knew all secrets. He saw him under the fig tree. He was God. Nathanael's call is just as clearly typical of Israel in the latter day. The allusion to the fig-tree confirms this. So does his confession: Rabbi, thou art the Son of God: thou art the King of Israel. (See Psalm 2) But the Lord tells him of greater things he, should see, and says to him, Verily, verily, I say unto you, henceforth (not "hereafter," but henceforth) ye shall see the heaven opened, and the angels of God ascending and descending on the Son of man. It is the wider, universal glory of the Son of man (according to Psalm 8); but the most striking part of it verified from that actual moment because of the glory of His person, which needed not the day of glory to command the attendance of the angels of God — this mark, as Son of man. (Verses 44-51)

On the third day is the marriage in Cana of Galilee, where was His mother, Jesus also, and His disciples. (John 2) The change of water into wine manifested His glory as the beginning of signs;

and He gave another in this early purging of the temple of Jerusalem. Thus we have traced, first, hearts not only attracted to Him, but fresh souls called to follow Him; then, in type, the call of Israel by-and-by; finally, the disappearance of the sign of moral purifying for the joy of the new covenant, when Messiah's time comes to bless the needy earth; but along with this the execution of judgment in Jerusalem, and its long defiled temple. All this clearly goes down to millennial days.

As a present fact, the Lord justifies the judicial act before their eyes by His relationship with God as His Father, and gives the Jews a sign in the temple of His body, as the witness of His resurrection power. "Destroy this temple, and in three days I will raise it up." He is ever God; He is the Son; He quickens and raises from the dead. Later He was determined to be Son of God with power by resurrection of the dead. They had eyes, but they saw not; ears had they, but they heard not, nor did they understand His glory. Alas! not the Jews only; for, as far as intelligence went, it was little better with the disciples till He rose from the dead. The resurrection of the Lord is not more truly a demonstration of His power and glory, than the only deliverance for disciples from the thraldom of Jewish influence. Without it there is no divine understanding of Christ, or of His word, or of Scripture. Further, it is connected intimately with the evidence of man's ruin by sin. Thus it is a kind of transitional fact for a most important part of our gospel, though still introductory. Christ was the true sanctuary, not that on which man had laboured so long in Jerusalem. Man might pull Him down — destroy Him, as far as man could, and surely to be the basis in God's hand of better blessing; but He was God, and in three days He would raise up this temple. Man was judged: another Man was there, the Lord from heaven, soon to stand in resurrection.

It is not now the revelation of God meeting man either in essential nature, or as manifested in flesh; nor is it the course of dispensational dealing presented in a parenthetic as well as mysterious form, beginning with John the Baptist's testimony, and going down to the millennium in the Son, full of grace and truth. It becomes a question of man's own condition, and how he stands in relation to the kingdom of God. This question is raised, or rather settled, by the Lord in Jerusalem, at the passover feast, where many believed on His name, beholding the signs He wrought. The dreadful truth comes out: The Lord did not trust Himself to them, because He knew all men. How withering the words! He had no need that any should testify of man, for He knew what was in man. It is not denunciation, but the most solemn sentence in the calmest manner. It was no longer a moot-point whether God could trust man; for, indeed, He could not. The question really is, whether man would trust God. Alas! he would not.

John 3 follows this up. God orders matters so that a favoured teacher of men, favoured as none others were in Israel, should come to Jesus by night. The Lord meets him at once with the strongest assertion of the absolute necessity that a man should be born anew in order to see the kingdom of God. Nicodemus, not understanding in the least such a want for himself, expresses his wonder, and hears our Lord increasing in the strength of the requirement. Except one were born of water and of the Spirit, he could not enter the kingdom of God. This was necessary for the kingdom of God; not for some special place of glory, but for any and every part of God's kingdom. Thus we have here the other side of the truth: not merely what God is in life and light, in grace and truth, as revealed in Christ coming down to man; but man is now judged in the very root of his nature, and proved to be entirely incapable, in his best state, of seeing or entering the kingdom of God. There is the need of another nature, and the only way in which this nature is communicated is by being born of water and the Spirit — the employment of the word of God in the quickening energy of the Holy Ghost. So only is man born of God. The Spirit of God uses that word; it is thus invariably in conversion. There is no other way in which the new nature is made good in a soul. Of course it is the revelation of Christ; but here He was simply revealing the sources of this indispensable new birth. There is no changing or bettering the old man; and, thanks be to God, the new does not degenerate or pass away. "That which is born of the flesh is flesh, and that which is born of the Spirit is spirit." (Verses 1-6)

But the Lord goes farther, and bids Nicodemus not wonder at His insisting on this need. As there is an absolute necessity on God's part that man should be thus born anew, so He lets him know there is an active grace of the Spirit, as the wind blows where it will, unknown and uncontrolled by man, for every one that is born of the Spirit, who is sovereign in operation. First, a new nature is insisted on — the Holy Ghost's quickening of each soul who is vitally related to God's kingdom; next, the Spirit of God takes an active part — not as source or character only, but acting sovereignly, which opens the way not only for a Jew, but for "every one." (Verses 7, 8)

It is hardly necessary to furnish detailed disproof of the crude, ill-considered notion (originated by the fathers), that baptism is in question. In truth, Christian baptism did not yet exist, but only such as the disciples used, like John the Baptist; it was not instituted of Christ till after His resurrection, as it sets forth His death. Had it been meant, it was no wonder that Nicodemus did not know how these things could be. But the Lord reproaches him, the master of Israel, with not knowing these things: that is, as a teacher, with Israel for his scholar, he ought to have known them objectively, at least, if not consciously. Isaiah 44:3, Isaiah 59:21, Ezekiel 36:25-27 ought to have made the Lord's meaning plain to an intelligent Jew. (Verse 10)

The Lord, it is true, could and did go farther than the prophets: even if He taught on the same theme, He could speak with conscious divine dignity and knowledge (not merely what was assigned to an instrument or messenger). "Verily, verily, I say unto thee, we speak that we do know, and testify that we have seen; and ye receive not our witness. If I have told you earthly things, and ye believe not, how shall ye believe, if I tell you of heavenly things? And no man hath ascended up to heaven, but he that came down from heaven, even the Son of man which is in heaven." (Verses 11-13) He (and He was not alone here) knew God, and the things of God, consciously in Himself, as surely as He knew all men, and what was in man objectively. He could, therefore, tell them of heavenly things as readily as of earthly things; but the incredulity about the latter, shown in the wondering ignorance of the new birth as a requisite for God's kingdom, proved it was useless to tell of the former. For He who spoke was divine. Nobody had gone up to heaven: God had taken more than one; but no one had gone there as of right. Jesus not only could go up, as He did later, but He had come down thence, and, even though man, He was the Son of man that is in heaven. He is a divine person; His manhood brought no attainder to His rights as God. Heavenly things, therefore, could not but be natural to Him, if one may so say.

Here the Lord introduces the cross. (Ver. 14, 15) It is not a question simply of the Son of God, nor is He spoken of here as the Word made flesh. But "as Moses lifted up the serpent in the wilderness, even so must (δεῖ) the Son of man be lifted up: that whosoever believeth in him should not perish, but have eternal life." As the new birth for the kingdom of God, so the cross is absolutely necessary for eternal life. In the Word was life, and the life was the light of men. It was not intended for other beings — it was God's free gift to man, to the believer, of course. Man, dead in sins, was the object of His grace; but then man's state was such, that it would have been derogatory to God had that life been communicated without the cross of Christ: the Son of man lifted up on it was the One in whom God dealt judicially with the evil estate of man, for the, full consequences of which He made Himself responsible. It would not suit God, if it would suit man, that He, seeing all, should just pronounce on man's corruption, and then forthwith let him off with a bare pardon. One must be born again. But even this sufficed not: the Son of man must be lifted up. It was impossible that there should not be righteous dealing with human evil against God, in its sources and its streams. Accordingly, if the law raised the question of righteousness in man, the cross of the Lord Jesus, typifying Him made sin, is the answer; and there has all been settled to the glory of God, the Lord Jesus having suffered all the inevitable consequences. Hence, then, we have the Lord Jesus alluding to this fresh necessity, if man was to be blessed according to God. "As Moses lifted up the serpent in the wilderness, even so must the Son of man be lifted up: that whosoever believeth in him should not perish, but have eternal life." But this, however worthy of God, and indispensable for man, could not of itself give an adequate expression of what God is; because in this alone, neither His own love nor the glory of His Son finds due display.

Hence, after having first unmistakably laid down the necessity of the cross, He next shows the grace that was manifested in the gift of Jesus. Here He is not portrayed as the Son of man who must be lifted up, but as the Son of God who was given. "For God," He says, "so loved the world, that he gave his only begotten Son, that whosoever believeth in him should not perish, but have eternal life." The one, like the other, contributes to this great end, whether the Son of man necessarily lifted up, or the only begotten Son of God given in His love. (Verse 16)

Let it not be passed by, that while the new birth or regeneration is declared to be essential to a part in the kingdom of God, the Lord in urging this intimates that He had not gone beyond the earthly things of that kingdom. Heavenly things are set in evident contradistinction, and link themselves immediately here, as everywhere, with the cross as their correlative. (See Heb. 12:2, Heb. 13:11-13) Again, let me just remark in passing, that although, no doubt, we may in a general way speak of those who partake of the new nature as having that life, yet the Holy Ghost refrains from predicating of any saints the full character of eternal life as a present thing until we have the cross of Christ laid (at least doctrinally) as the ground of it. But when the Lord speaks of His cross, and not God's judicial requirements only, but the gift of Himself in His true personal glory as the occasion for the grace of God to display itself to the utmost, then, and not till then, do we hear of eternal life, and this connected with both these points of view. The chapter pursues this subject, showing that it is not only God who thus deals — first, with the necessity of man before His own immutable nature; next, blessing according to the riches of His grace — but, further, that man's state morally is detected yet more awfully in presence of such grace as well as holiness in Christ. "For God sent not his Son into the world to judge the world; but that the world through him might be saved." (Ver. 17) This decides all before the execution of judgment, Every man's lot is made manifest by his attitude toward God's testimony concerning His Son. "He that believeth on him is not judged: but he that believeth not is judged already, because he hath not believed in the name of the only begotten Son of God." (Ver. 19) Other things, the merest trifles, may serve to indicate a man's condition; but a new responsibility is created by this infinite display of divine goodness in Christ, and the evidence is decisive and final, that the unbeliever is already judged before God. "And this is the judgment, that light is come into the world, and men loved darkness rather than light, because their deeds were evil. For every one that doeth evil hateth the light, neither cometh to the light, lest his deeds should be reproved. But he that doeth truth cometh to the light, that his deeds may be made manifest, that they are wrought in God." (Verses 20, 21)

The Lord and the disciples are next seen in the country district, not far, it would seem, from John, who was baptizing as they were. The disciples of John dispute with a Jew about purification; but John himself renders a bright witness to the glory of the Lord Jesus. In vain did any come to the Baptist to report the widening circle around Christ. He bows to, as he explains, the sovereign will of God. He reminds them of his previous disclaimer of any place beyond one sent before Jesus. His joy was that of a friend of the Bridegroom (to whom, not to him, the bride belonged), and now fulfilled as he heard the Bridegroom's voice. "He must, increase, but I decrease." Blessed servant he of an infinitely blessed and blessing Master! Then (ver. 31-36) he speaks of His person in contrast with himself and all; of His testimony and of the result, both as to His own glory, and consequently also for the believer on, and the rejecter of, the Son. He that comes from above — from heaven — is above all. Such was Jesus in person, contrasted with all who belong to the earth. Just as distinct and beyond comparison is His testimony who, coming from heaven and above all, testifies what He saw and heard, however it might be rejected. But see the blessed fruit of receiving it. "He that hath received his testimony hath set to his seal that God is true. For he whom God hath sent speaketh the words of God: for God giveth not the Spirit by measure unto him." I apprehend the words the Authorised Version gives in italics should disappear. The addition of "unto him" detracts, to my mind, from the exceeding preciousness of what seems to be, at least, left open. For the astonishing thought is, not merely that Jesus receives the Holy Ghost without measure, but that God gives the Spirit also, and not by measure, through Him to others. In the beginning of the chapter it was rather an essential indispensable action of the Holy Ghost required; here it is the privilege of the Holy Ghost given. No doubt Jesus Himself had the Holy Ghost given to Him, as it was meet that He in all things should have the pre-eminence; but it shows yet more both the personal glory of Christ and the efficacy of His work, that He now gives the same Spirit to those who receive His testimony, and set to their seal that God is true. How singularly is the glory of the Lord Jesus thus viewed, as invested with the testimony of God and its crown! What more glorious proof than that the Holy Ghost is given — not a certain defined power or gift, but the Holy Ghost Himself; for God gives not the Spirit by measure!

All is fitly closed by the declaration, that "the Father loveth the Son, and hath given all things into his hand." It is not merely or most of all a great prophet or witness: He is the Son; and the Father has given all things to be in His hand. There is the nicest care to maintain His personal glory, no matter what the subject may be. The results for the believer or unbeliever are eternal in good or in evil. He that believes on the Son has everlasting life; and he that disobeys the Son, in the sense of not being subject to His person, "shall not see life; but the wrath of God abideth on him" Such is the issue of the Son of God present in this world — an everlasting one for every man, flowing from the glory of His person, the character of His testimony, and the Father's counsels respecting Him. The effect is thus final, even as His person, witness, and glory are divine.

The chapters we have had before us (John 1-3) are thus evidently an introduction: God revealed not in the Word alone, but in the Word made flesh, in the Son who declared the Father; His work, as God's Lamb, for the world, and His power by the Holy Ghost in man; then viewed as the centre of gathering, as the path to follow, and as the object even for the attendance of God's angels, the heaven being opened, and Jesus — not the Son of God and King of Israel only, but the Son of man — object of God's counsels. This will be displayed in the millennium, when the marriage will be celebrated, as well as the judgment executed (Jerusalem and its temple being the central point then). This, of course, supposes the setting aside of Jerusalem, its people and house, as they now are, and is justified by the great fact of Christ's death and resurrection, which is the key to all, though not yet intelligible even to the disciples. This brings in the great counterpart truth, that even God present on earth and made flesh is not enough. Man is morally judged. One must be born again for God's kingdom — a Jew for what was promised him, like another. But the Spirit would not confine His operations to such bounds, but go out freely like the wind. Nor would the rejected Christ, the Son of man; for if lifted up on the cross, instead of having the throne of David, the result would be not merely earthly blessing for His people according to prophecy, but eternal life for the believer, whoever. he might be; and this, too, as the expression of the true and full grace of God in His only-begotten Son given. John then declared his own waning before Christ, as we have seen, the issues of whose testimony, believed or not, are eternal; and this founded on the revelation of His glorious person as man and to man here below.

John 4 presents the Lord Jesus outside Jerusalem — outside the people of promise — among Samaritans, with whom Jews had no intercourse. Pharisaic jealousy had wrought; and Jesus, wearied, sat thus at the fountain of Jacob's well in Sychar. (Ver. 1-6) What a picture of rejection and humiliation! Nor was it yet complete. For if, on the one side, God has taken care to let us see already the glory of the Son, and the grace of which He was full, on the other side, all shines out the more marvellously when we know how He dealt with a woman of Samaria, sinful and degraded. Here was a meeting, indeed, between such an one and Him, the Son, true God and eternal life. Grace begins, glory descends; "Jesus saith unto her, give me to drink." (Verse 1) It was strange to her that a Jew should thus humble himself: what would it have been, had she seen in Him Jesus the Son of God? "Jesus answered and said unto her, if thou knewest the gift of God, and who it is that saith to thee, give me to drink; thou wouldest have asked of him, and he would have given thee living water." (Verse 10) Infinite grace! infinite truth! and the more manifest from His lips to one who was a real impersonation of sin, misery, blindness, degradation. But this is not the question of grace: not what she was, but what He is who was there to win and bless her, manifesting God and the Father withal, practically and in detail. Surely He was there, a weary man outside Judaism; but God, the God of all grace, who humbled Himself to ask a drink of water of her, that He might give the richest and most enduring gift, even water which, once drank, leaves no thirst for ever and ever — yea, is in him who drinks a fountain of water springing up unto everlasting life. Thus the Holy Ghost, given by the Son in humiliation (according to God, not acting on law, but according to the gift of grace in the gospel), was fully set forth; but the woman, though interested, and asking, only apprehended a boon for this life to save herself trouble here below. This gives occasion to Jesus to teach us the lesson that conscience must be reached, and sense of sin produced, before grace is understood and brings forth fruit. This He does in verses 16-19. Her life is laid before her by His voice, and she confesses to Him that God Himself spoke to her in His words: "Sir [said she], I perceive that thou art a prophet." If she turned aside to questions of religion, with a mixture of desire to learn what had concerned and perplexed her, and of willingness to escape such a searching of her ways and heart, He did not refrain graciously to vouchsafe the revelation of God, that earthly worship was doomed, that the Father was to be worshipped, not an Unknown. And while He does not hide the privilege of the Jews, He nevertheless proclaims that "the hour cometh, and now is, when the true worshippers shall worship the Father in spirit and in truth: for the Father seeketh such to worship him. God is a Spirit: and they that worship him must worship him in spirit and in truth." This brings all to a point; for the woman says, "I know that Messiah cometh, which is called Christ: when he is come, he will tell us all things." And Jesus answers, "I that speak unto thee am he." The disciples come; the woman goes into the city, leaving her waterpot, but carrying with her the unspeakable gift of God. Her testimony bore the impress of what had penetrated her soul, and would make way for all the rest in due time. "Come, see a man that told me all things that ever I did: is not this the Christ?" "Whosoever believeth that Jesus is the Christ is born of God." It was much, yet was it little of the glory that was His; but at least it was real; and to the one that has shall be given. (Verses 20-30)

The disciples marvelled that He spoke with the woman. How little they conceived of what was then said and done! "Master, eat," said they. "But He said to them, I have meat to eat that ye know not of." They entered not into His words more than His grace, but thought and spoke, like the Samaritan woman, about things of this life. Jesus explains: "My meat is to do the will of him that sent me, and to finish his work. Say not ye, There are yet four months, and then cometh harvest? behold, I say unto you, Lift up your eyes, and look on the fields; for they are white already to harvest. And he that reapeth receiveth wages, and gathereth fruit unto life eternal: that both he that soweth and he that reapeth may rejoice together. And herein is that true saying, One soweth, and another reapeth. I sent you to reap that whereon ye bestowed no labour: other men laboured, and ye are entered into their labours." (Verses 31-38)

Thus a despised Christ is not merely a crucified Son of man, and given Son of God, as in John 3, but Himself a divine giver in communion with the Father, and in the power of the Holy Ghost who is given to the believer, the source of worship, as their God and Father is its object for the worshippers in spirit and truth (though surely not to the exclusion of the Son, Heb. 1). So it must be now; for God is revealed; and the Father in grace seeks true worshippers (be they Samaritans or Jews) to worship Him. Here, accordingly, it is not so much the means by which life is communicated, as the revelation of the full blessing of grace and communion with the Father and His Son by the Holy Ghost, in whom we are blessed. Hence it is that here the Son, according to the grace of God the Father, gives the Holy Ghost — eternal life in the power of the Spirit. It is not simply the new birth such as a saint might, and always must, have had, in order to vital relations with God at any time. Here, in suited circumstances to render the thought and way of God unmistakable, pure and boundless grace takes its own sovereign course, suitable to the love and personal glory of Christ. For if the Son (cast out, we may say, in principle from Judaism) visited Samaria, and deigned to talk with one of the most worthless of that worthless race, it could not be a mere rehearsal of what

others did. Not Jacob was there, but the Son of God in nothing but grace; and thus to the Samaritan woman, not to the teachers of Israel, are made those wonderful communications which unfold to us with incomparable depth and beauty the real source, power, and character of that worship which supersedes, not merely schismatic and rebellious Samaria, but Judaism at its best. For evidently it is the theme of worship in its Christian fulness, the fruit of the manifestation of God, and of the Father known in grace. And worship is viewed both in moral nature and in the joy of communion — doubly. First, we must worship, if at all, in spirit and in truth. This is indispensable; for God is a Spirit, and so it cannot but be. Besides this, goodness overflows, in that the Father is gathering children, and making worshippers. The Father seeks worshippers. What love! In short, the riches of God's grace are here according to the glory of the Son, and in the power of the Holy Ghost. Hence the Lord, while fully owning the labours of all preceding labourers, has before His eyes the whole boundless expanse of grace, the mighty harvest which His apostles were to reap in due time. It is thus strikingly an anticipation of the result in glory. Meanwhile, for Christian worship, the hour was coming and in principle come, because He was there; and He who vindicated salvation as of the Jews, proves that it is now for Samaritans, or any who believed on account of His word. Without sign, prodigy, or miracle, in this village of Samaria Jesus was heard, known, confessed as truly the Saviour of the world ("the Christ" being absent in the best authorities, ver. 42). The Jews, with all their privileges, were strangers here. They knew what they worshipped, but not the Father, nor were they "true." No such sounds, no such realities were ever heard or known in Israel. How were they not enjoyed in despised Samaria — those two days with the Son of God among them! It was meet that so it should be; for, as a question of right, none could claim; and grace surpasses all expectation or thought of man, most of all of men accustomed to a round of religious ceremonial. Christ did not wait till the time was fully come for the old things to pass away, and all to be made new. His own love and person were warrant enough for the simple to lift the veil for a season, and fill the hearts which had received Himself into the conscious enjoyment of divine grace, and of Him who revealed it to them. It was but preliminary, of course; still it was a deep reality, the then present grace in the person of the Son, the Saviour of the world, who filled their once dark hearts with light and joy.

The close of the chapter shows us the Lord in Galilee. But there was this difference from the former occasion, that, at the marriage in Cana (John 2), the change of the water into wine was clearly millennial in its typical aspect. The healing of the courtier's son, sick and ready to die, is witness of what the Lord was actually doing among the despised of Israel. It is there that we found the Lord, in the other synoptic gospels, fulfilling His ordinary ministry. John gives us this point of contact with them, though in an incident peculiar to himself. It is our evangelist's way of indicating His Galilean sojourn; and this miracle is the particular subject that John was led by the Holy Ghost to take up. Thus, as in the former case the Lord's dealing in Galilee was a type of the future, this appears to be significant of His then present path of grace in that despised quarter of the land. The looking for signs and wonders is rebuked; but mortality is arrested. His corporeal presence was not necessary; His word was enough. The contrasts are as strong, at least, as the resemblance with the healing of the centurion's servant in Matt. 13 and Luke 7, which some ancients and moderns have confounded with this, as they did Mary's anointing of Jesus with the sinful woman's in Luke 7.

One of the peculiarities of our gospel is, that we see the Lord from time to time (and, indeed, chiefly) in or near Jerusalem. This is the more striking, because, as we have seen, the world and Israel, rejecting Him, are also themselves, as such, rejected from the first. The truth is, the design of manifesting His glory governs all; place or people was a matter of no consequence.

Here (John 5) the first view given of Christ is His person in contrast with the law. Man, under law, proved powerless; and the greater the need, the less the ability to avail himself of such merciful intervention as God still, from time to time, kept up throughout the legal system. The same God who did not leave Himself without witness among the heathen, doing good, and giving from heaven rain and fruitful seasons, did not fail, in the low estate of the Jews, to work by providential power at intervals; and, by the troubled waters of Bethesda, invited the sick, and healed the first who stepped in of whatever disease he had. In the five porches, then, of this pool lay a great multitude of sick, blind, lame, withered, waiting for the moving of the water. But there was a man who had been infirm for thirty and eight years. Jesus saw the man, and knowing that he was long thus, prompts the desire of healing, but brings out the despondency of unbelief. How truly it is man under law! Not only is there no healing to be extracted from the law by a sinner, but the law makes more evident the disease, if it does not also aggravate the symptoms. The law works no deliverance; it puts a man in chains, prison, darkness, and under condemnation; it renders him a patient, or a criminal incompetent to avail himself of the displays of God's goodness. God never left Himself without witness; He did not even among the Gentiles, surely yet less in Israel. Still, such is the effect on man under law, that he could not take advantage of an adequate remedy. (Verses 1-7)

On the other hand, the Lord speaks but the word: "Rise, take up thy couch and walk." The result immediately follows. It was sabbath-day. The Jews, then, who could not help, and pitied not their fellow in his long infirmity and disappointment, are scandalized to see him, safe and sound, carrying his couch on that day. But they learn that it was his divine Physician who had not only healed, but so directed him. At once their malice drops the beneficent power of God in the case, provoked at the fancied wrong done to the seventh day. (Verses 8-12)

But were the Jews mistaken after all in thinking that the seal of the first covenant was virtually broken in that deliberate word and warranty of Jesus? He could have healed the man without the smallest outward act to shock their zeal for the law. Expressly had He told the man to take up his couch and walk, as well as to rise. There was purpose in it. There was sentence of death pronounced on their system, and they felt accordingly. The man could not tell the Jews the name of his benefactor. But Jesus finds him in the temple, and said, "Behold, thou art made whole:

sin no more, lest a worse thing come unto thee." The man went off, and told the Jews that it was Jesus: and for this they persecuted Him, because He had done these things on the sabbath. (Verses 13-16)

A graver issue, however, was to be tried; for Jesus answered them, My Father worketh hitherto, and I work. For this, therefore, the Jews sought the more to kill Him; — because He added the greater offence of making Himself equal with God, by saying that God was His own Father. (Verses 17, 18)

Thus, in His person, as well as in His work, they joined issue. Nor could any question be more momentous. If He spoke the truth, they were blasphemers. But how precious the grace, in presence of their hatred and proud self-complacency! "My Father worketh hitherto, and I work." They had no common thoughts, feelings, or ways with the Father and the Son. Were the Jews zealously keeping the sabbath? The Father and the Son were at work. How could either light or love rest in a scene of sin, darkness, and misery?

Did they charge Jesus with self-exaltation? No charge could be remoter from the truth. Though He could not, would not deny Himself (and He was the Son, and Word, and God), yet had He taken the place of a man, of a servant. Jesus, therefore, answered, "Verily, verily, I say unto you, The Son can do nothing of himself, but what he seeth the Father do: for what things soever he doeth, these also doeth the Son likewise. For the Father loveth the Son, and showeth him all things that himself doeth: and he will show him greater works than these, that ye may marvel. For as the Father raiseth up the dead, and quickeneth them; even so the Son quickeneth whom he will. For the Father judgeth no man, but hath committed all judgment unto the Son: that all men should honour the Son, even as they honour the Father. He that honoureth not the Son honoureth not the Father which hath sent him. Verily, verily, I say unto you, He that heareth my word, and believeth on him that sent me, hath everlasting life, and shall not come into judgment; but is passed from death unto life. Verily, verily, I say unto you, the hour is coming, and now is, when the dead shall hear the voice of the Son of God: and they that hear shall live. For as the Father hath life in himself, so hath he given to the Son to have life in himself; and hath given him authority to execute judgment also, because he is the Son of man. Marvel not at this: for the hour is coming, in the which all that are in the graves shall hear his voice, and shall come forth; they that have done good, unto the resurrection of life; and they that have done evil, unto the resurrection of judgment." (Ver. 19-29)

It is evident, then, that the Lord presents life in Himself as the true want of man, who was not merely infirm but dead. Law, means, ordinances, could not meet the need — no pool, nor angel — nothing but the Son working in grace, the Son quickening. Governmental healing even from Him might only end in "some worse thing" coming. through "sin." Life out of death was wanted by man, such as he is; and this the Father is giving in the Son. Whosoever denieth the Son hath not the Father; he that acknowledgeth the Son hath the Father also. This is the truth; but the Jews had the law, and hated the truth. Could they, then, reject the Son, and merely miss this infinite blessing of life in Him? Nay, the Father has given all judgment to the Son. He will have all honour the Son, even as Himself

And as life is in the person of the Son, so God in sending Him meant not that the smallest uncertainty should exist for aught so momentous. He would have every soul to know assuredly how he stands for eternity as well as now. There is but one unfailing test — the Son of God — God's testimony to Him. Therefore, it seems to me, He adds verse 24. It is not a question of the law, but of hearing Christ's word, and believing Him who sent Christ: he that does so has everlasting life, and shall not come into judgment; but is passed from death unto life. The Word, God (and only begotten Son in the Father's bosom), He was eternally — Son of God, too, as born into the world. Was this false and blasphemous in their eyes? They could not deny Him to be man

— Son of man. Nay, therefore it was they, reasoning, denied Him to be God. Let them learn, then, that as Son of man (for which nature they despised Him, and denied His essential personal glory) He will judge; and this judgment will be no passing visitation, such as God has accomplished by angels or men in times past. The judgment, all of it, whether for quick or dead, is consigned to Him, because He is Son of man. Such is God's vindication of His outraged rights; and the judgment will be proportionate to the glory that has been set at nought.

Thus solemnly does the meek Lord Jesus unfold these two truths. In Him was life for this scene of death; and it is of faith that it might be by grace. This only secures His honour in those that believe God's testimony to Him, the Son of God; and to these He gives life, everlasting life now, and exemption from judgment, in this acting in communion with the Father. And in this He is sovereign. The Son gives life, as the Father does; and not merely to whom the Father will, but to whom He will. Nevertheless, the Son had taken the place of being the sent One, the place of subordination in the earth, in which He would say, "My Father is greater than I." And He did accept that place thoroughly, and in all its consequences. But let them beware how they perverted it. Granted He was the Son of man; but as such, He had all judgment given Him, and would judge. Thus in one way or the other all must honour the Son. The Father did not judge, but committed all judgment into the hands of the Son, because He is the Son of man. It was not the time now to demonstrate in public power these coming, yea, then present truths. The hour was one for faith, or unbelief. Did the dead (for so men are treated, not as alive under law) — did they hear the voice of the Son of God? Such shall live. For though the Son (that eternal life who was with the Father) was a man, in that very position had the Father given Him to have life in Himself, and to execute judgment also, because He is Son of man. Judgment is the alternative for man: for God it is the resource to make good the glory of the Son, and in that nature, in and for which man — blind to his own highest dignity — dares to despise Him. Two resurrections, one of life, and another of judgment, would be the manifestation of faith and unbelief, or rather, of those who believe, and of those who reject the Son. They were not to wonder then at what He says and does now; for an hour was coming in which all that are in the graves shall hear His voice, and shall come forth; those that have done good to resurrection of life, and those that have done evil to resurrection of judgment. This would make all manifest. Now it is that the great question is decided; now it is that a man receives or refuses Christ. If he receives Him, it is everlasting life, and Christ is thus honoured by him; if not, judgment remains which will compel the honour of Christ, but to his own ruin for ever. Resurrection will be the proof; the two-fold rising of the dead, not one, but two resurrections. Life — resurrection will display how little they had to be ashamed of, who believed the record given of His Son; the resurrection of judgment will make but too plain, to those who despised the Lord, both His honour and their sin and shame.

As this chapter sets forth the Lord Jesus with singular fulness of glory, on the side both of His Godhead and of His manhood, so it closes with the most varied and remarkable testimonies God has given to us, that there may be no excuse. So bright was His glory, so concerned was the Father in maintaining it, so immense the blessing if received, so tremendous the stake involved in its loss, that God vouchsafed the amplest and clearest witnesses. If He judges, it is not without full warning. Accordingly, there is a four-fold testimony to Jesus: the testimony of John the Baptist; the Lord's own works; the voice of the Father from heaven; and finally, the written word which the Jews had in their own hands. To this last the Lord attaches the deepest importance. This testimony differs from the rest in having a more permanent character. Scripture is, or may be, before man always. It is not a message or a sign, however significant at the moment, which passes away as soon as heard or seen. As a weapon of conviction, most justly had it in the mind of the Lord Jesus the weightiest place, little as man thinks now-a-days of it. The issue of all is, that the will of man is the real cause and spring of enmity. "Ye will not come to me that ye might have life." it was no lack of testimony; their will was for present honour, and hostile to the glory of the only God. They would fall a prey to Antichrist, and meanwhile are accused of Moses, in whom they trusted, without believing him; else they would have believed Christ, of whom he wrote.

In John 6 our Lord sets aside Israel in another point of view. Not only man under law has no health, but he has no strength to avail himself of the blessing that God holds out. Nothing less than everlasting life in Christ can deliver: otherwise there remains judgment. Here the Lord was really owned by the multitudes as the great Prophet that should come; and this in consequence of His works, especially that one which Scripture itself had connected with the Son of David. (Ps. 132) Then they wanted to make Him a king. It seemed natural: He had fed the poor with bread, and why should not He take His place on the throne? This the Lord refuses, and goes up the mountain to pray, His disciples being meanwhile exposed to a storm on the lake, and straining after the desired haven till He rejoins them, when immediately the ship was at the land whither they went. (Verses 1-21)

The Lord, in the latter part of the chapter (verses 27-58), contrasts the presentation of the truth of God in His person and work with all that pertained to the promises of Messiah. It is not that He denies the truth of what they were thus desiring and attached to. Indeed, He was the great Prophet, as He was the great King, and as He is now the great Priest on high. Still the Lord refused the crown then: it was not the time or state for His reign. Deeper questions demanded solution. A greater work was in hand; and this, as the rest of the chapter shows us, not a Messiah lifted up, but the true bread given — He who comes down out of heaven, and gives life to the world; a dying, not a reigning, Son of man. It is His person as incarnate first, then in redemption giving His flesh to be eaten and His blood to be drank. Thus former things pass away; the old man is judged, dead, and clean gone. A second and wholly new man appears — the bread of God, not of man, but for men. The character is wholly different from the position and glory of Messiah in Israel, according to promise and prophecy. Indeed, it is the total eclipse, not merely of law and remedial mercies, but even of promised Messianic glory, by everlasting life and resurrection at the last day. Christ here, it will be noticed, is not so much the quickening agent as Son of God (John 5), but the object of faith as Son of man — first incarnate, to be eaten; then dying and giving His flesh to be eaten, and His blood to be drank. Thus we feed on Him and drink into Him, as man, unto life — everlasting life in Him.

This last is the figure of a truth deeper than incarnation, and clearly means communion with His death. They had stumbled before, and the Lord brought in not alone His person, as the Word made flesh, presented for man now to receive and enjoy; but unless they ate the flesh, and drank the blood of the Son of man, they had no life in them. There He supposes His full rejection and death. He speaks of Himself as the Son of man in death; for there could be no eating of His flesh, no drinking of His blood, as a living man. Thus it is not only the person of our Lord viewed as divine, and coming down into the world. He who, living, was received for eternal life, is our meat and drink in dying, and gives us communion with His death. Thus, in fact, we have the Lord setting aside what was merely Messianic by the grand truths of the incarnation, and, above all, of the atonement, with which man must have vital association: he must eat — yea, eat and drink. This language is said of both, but most strongly of the latter. And so, in fact, it was and is. He who owns the reality of Christ's incarnation, receives most thankfully and adoringly from God the truth of redemption; he, on the contrary, who stumbles at redemption, has not really taken in the incarnation according to God's mind. If a man looks at the Lord Jesus as One who entered the world in a general way, and calls this the incarnation, he will surely stumble over the cross. If, on the contrary, a soul has been taught of God the glory of the person of Him who was made flesh, he receives in all simplicity, and rejoices in, the glorious truth, that He who was made flesh was not made flesh only to this end, but rather as a step toward another and deeper work — the glorifying God, and becoming our food, in death. Such are the grand emphatic points to which the Lord leads.

But the chapter does not close without a further contrast. (Verses 59-71) What and if they should see Him, who came down and died in this world, ascend up where He was before? All is in the character of the Son of man. The Lord Jesus did, without question, take humanity in His person into that glory which He so well knew as the Son of the Father.

On this basis John 7 proceeds. The brethren of the Lord Jesus, who could see the astonishing power that was in Him, but whose hearts were carnal, at once discerned that it might be an uncommon good thing for them, as well as for Him, in this world. It was worldliness in its worst shape, even to the point of turning the glory of Christ to a present account. Why should He not show Himself to the world? (Verses 3-5) The Lord intimates the impossibility of anticipating the time of God; but then He does it as connected with His own personal glory. Then He rebukes the carnality of His brethren. If His time was not yet come, their time was always ready. (Ver. 6-8) They belonged to the world. They spoke of the world; the world might hear them. As to Himself, He does not go at that time to the feast of tabernacles; but later on He goes up "not openly, but as it were in secret" (verse 10), and taught. They wonder, as they had murmured before (12-15); but Jesus shows that the desire to do God's will is the condition of spiritual understanding. (Verses 16-18) , The Jews kept not the law) and wished to kill Him who healed man in divine love. (Verses 19-23) What judgment could be less righteous? (Ver. 24) They reason and are in utter uncertainty. (Ver. 25-31) He is going where they cannot come, and never guessed (for unbelief thinks of the dispersed among the Greeks — of anything rather than of God). (Verses 33-36) Jesus was returning to Him that sent Him, and the Holy Ghost would be given. So on the last day, that great day of the feast (the eighth day, which witnessed of a resurrection glory outside this creation, now to be made good in the power of the Spirit before anything appears to sight), the Lord stands and cries, saying, "If any man thirst, let him come unto me and drink." (Ver. 37) It is not a question of eating the bread of God, or, when Christ died, of eating His flesh and drinking His blood. Here, "If any man thirst, let him come unto me and drink." Just as in John 4, so here it is a question of power in the Holy Ghost, and not simply of Christ's person. "He that believeth on me, as the scripture hath said, out of his belly shall flow rivers of living water." (Ver. 38) And then we have the comment of the Holy Ghost: "(But this spake he of the Spirit, which they that believe on him should receive: for the Holy ghost was not yet given; because that Jesus was not yet glorified)" There is, first, the thirsty soul coming to Jesus and drinking; then there is the power of the Spirit flowing forth from the inner man of the believer in refreshment to others. (Verse 39)

Nothing can be simpler than this. Details are not called for now, but just the outline of the truth. But what we learn is, that our Lord (viewed as having entered into heaven as man on the ground of redemption, i.e., ascended, after having passed through death, into glory) from that glory confers meanwhile the Holy Ghost on him that believes, instead of bringing in at once the final feast of gladness for the Jews and the world, as He will do by-and-by when the anti-typical harvest and vintage has been fulfilled. Thus it is not the Spirit of God simply giving a new nature; neither is it the Holy Ghost given as the power of worship and communion with His God and Father. This we have had fully before. Now, it is the Holy Ghost in the power that gives rivers of living water flowing out, and this bound up with, and consequent on, His being man in glory. Till then the Holy Ghost could not be so given — only when Jesus was glorified, after redemption was a fact. What can be more evident, or more instructive? It is the final setting aside of Judaism then, whose characteristic hope was the display of power and rest in the world. But here these streams of the Spirit are substituted for the feast of tabernacles, which cannot be accomplished till Christ come from heaven and show Himself to the world; for this time was not yet come. Rest is not the question now at all; but the flow of the Spirit's power while Jesus is on high. In a certain sense, the principle of John 4 was made true in the woman of Samaria, and in others who received Christ then. The person of the Son was there the object of divine and overflowing joy even then, although, of course, in the full sense of the word, the Holy Ghost might not be given to be the power of it for some time later; but still the object of worship was there revealing the Father; but John 7 supposes Him to be gone up to heaven, before He from heaven communicates the Holy Ghost, who should be (not here, as Israel had a rock with water to drink of in the wilderness outside themselves, nor even as a fountain springing up within the believer, but) as rivers flowing out. How blessed the contrast with the people's state depicted in this chapter, tossed about by every wind of doctrine, looking to "letters," rulers, and Pharisees, perplexed about the Christ, but without righteous judgment, assurance, or enjoyment! Nicodemus remonstrates but is spurned; all retire to their home — Jesus, who had none, to the mount of Olives. (Verses 40-53)

This closes the various aspects of the Lord Jesus, completely blotting out Judaism, viewed as resting in a system of law and ordinances, as looking to a Messiah with present ease, and as hoping for the display of Messianic glory then in the world. The Lord Jesus presents Himself as putting an end to all this now for the Christian, though, of course, every word God has promised, as well as threatened, remains to be accomplished in Israel by-and-by; for Scripture cannot be broken; and what the mouth of the Lord has said awaits its fulfilment in its due sphere and season.

JOHN 8-14

The point at which we have arrived gives me an opportunity of saying a little on the beginning of this chapter, and the end of the last; for it is well known that many men, and, I am sorry to add, not a few Christians, have allowed appearances to weigh against John 7:53 — John 8:11 — a very precious portion of God's word. The fact is, that the paragraph of the convicted adulteress has been either simply left out in some copies of Scripture, or a blank equivalent to it appears, or it is given with marks of doubt and a good deal of variety of reading, or it is put in elsewhere. This, with many alleged verbal peculiarities, acted on the minds of a considerable number, and led them to question its title to a place in the genuine gospel of John. I do not think that the objections usually raised are here understated. Nevertheless, mature as well as minute consideration of them fails to raise the slightest doubt in my own mind, and therefore to me it seems so much the more a duty to defend it, where the alternative is a dishonour to what I believe God has given us.

In its favour are the strongest possible proofs from such a character in itself, and such suitability to the context, as no forgery could ever boast. And these moral or spiritual indications (though, of course, only to such as are capable of apprehending and enjoying God's mind) are incomparably graver and more conclusive than any evidence of an external sort. Not that the external evidence is really weak, far from it. That which gives such an appearance is capable of reasonable, unforced, and even of what seems almost to amount to an historical solution. The meddling was probably due to human motives — no uncommon thing in ancient or modern times. With good and with bad intentions men have often tried to mend the word of God. Superstitious persons, unable to enter into its beauty, and anxious after the good opinion of the world, were afraid to trust the truth which Christ was here setting forth in deed. Augustine[4], an unimpeachable witness of facts, nearly as old as the most ancient manuscripts which omit the paragraph, tells us that it was from ethical difficulties some dropped this section out of their copies. We know for certain that dogmatic motives similarly influenced some in Luke 22:42, 43. One of the considerations, adverted to already, ought to weigh exceedingly with the believer. The account, I shall show, is exactly in harmony with the Scripture that follows it — not less so than the Lord's refusal to go up to the feast and show Himself to the world, with His words which follow on the gift of the Holy Ghost in John 7; or, again, the miracle of the miraculous bread, with the discourse appended on the needed food for the Christian in John 6. In a word, there is here, as there, an indissoluble link of connected truth between the facts related and the communication our Lord makes afterwards in each instance respectively.

For, let me ask, what is the salient divine principle which runs through our Lord's conduct and language when the scribes and Pharisees confront Him with the woman taken in adultery? A flagrant case of sin was produced. They manifest no holy hatred of the evil, and certainly feel no pity for the sinner. "They say unto him, Master, this woman was taken in adultery, in the very act. Now Moses in the law commanded us, that such should be stoned: but what sayest thou?[5] This they said, tempting him, that

---

[4] The suspicion that some weak believers or enemies of the faith omitted the section, as the Bishop of Hippo suggests, would expose the passage to be tampered with. It is very likely that the Christians who read the Shepherd of Hermas in their public services would omit John 8:1-11. Similar unbelief inclines critical judgment in that direction now. Judgment of facts is apt to be swayed and formed by the will.

[5] It is the remark of a critic unfriendly to the passage, that this question belongs to the last days of our Lord's ministry, and cannot well be introduced chronologically here. Unconsciously, however, this is really a strong confirmation; for morally John starts with the rejection of Jesus, and gives at the beginning even (as in the cleansing of the temple) similar truths to those which the rest attest at the close.

they might have to accuse him." Their hope was to ensnare Christ, and to leave Him only a choice of difficulties: either a useless repetition of the law of Moses, or open opposition to the law. If the latter, would it not prove Him God's adversary? If the former, would He not forfeit all His pretensions to grace? For they were well aware, that in all the ways and language of Christ, there was that which totally differed from the law and all before Him. Indeed, they counted on His grace, though they felt it not, relished it not, in no way valued it as of God; but still they so expected grace in our Lord's dealing with so heinous a sinner as the one before them, that they hoped thereby to commit Him fatally in the eyes of men. Enmity to His person was their motive. To agree with Moses or to annul him seemed to them inevitable, and almost equally prejudicial to the claims of Jesus. No doubt, they most expected that our Lord in His grace would oppose the law, and thus put Himself and grace in the wrong.

But the fact is, the grace of God never conflicts with His law, but, on the contrary, maintains its authority in its own sphere. There is nothing which clears, establishes, and vindicates the law, and every other principle of God, so truly as His grace. Even the proprieties of nature were never so made good as when the Lord manifested grace on the earth. Take, for instance, His ways in Matthew 19. Whoever developed God's idea and will in marriage as Christ did? Who cast light on the value of a little child till Christ did? When a man left Himself, who could look so wistfully and with such love upon him as Jesus? Grace therefore is in no way inconsistent with, but maintains obligations at their true height. It is precisely thus, only still more gloriously, with our Lord's conduct on this occasion; for He weakens not in the least either the law or its sanctions, but contrariwise sheds around divine light in His own words and ways, and even applies the law with convincing power, not merely to the convicted criminal, but to the more hidden guilt of her accusers. Not a single self-righteous soul was left in that all-searching presence — none indeed of those who came about the matter, except the woman herself.

Choose for me in all Scripture a preface of fact so suited to the doctrine of the chapter that follows. The whole chapter, from first to last, beams with light — the light of God and of His word in the person of Jesus. Is not this undeniably what comes out in the opening incident? Does not Christ present Himself in discourse just after as the light of the world (so continually in John), as God's light by His word in Himself, infinitely superior even to law, and yet at the same time giving the law its fullest authority? Only a divine person could thus put and keep everything in its due place; only a divine person could act in perfect grace, but at the same time maintain immaculate holiness, and so much the more because it was in One full of grace.

This is just what the Lord does. Therefore, when the charge was brought thus heartlessly against outward evil, He simply stoops down, and with His finger writes on the ground. He allowed them to think of the circumstances, of themselves, and of Him. As they still continued asking, He lifted up Himself, and said unto them, "He that is without sin among you, let him first cast the stone at her." And again, stooping down, He writes on the round. (Verses 6-8) The first act allows the full iniquity of their aim to be realized. They hoped, no doubt, it might be an insuperable difficulty to Him. They had time to weigh what they had said and were seeking. When they continued to ask, and He lifted Himself up and spoke to them those memorable words, He again stoops, that they might weigh them in their consciences. It was the light of God cast on their thoughts, words, and life. The words were few, simple, and self-evidencing. He that is without sin among you, let him first cast the stone at her." The effect was immediate and complete. His words penetrated to the heart. Why did not some of the witnesses rise and do the office? What! not one? "They which heard it, being convicted by their own conscience, went out one by one, beginning at the eldest, even unto the last.; and Jesus was left alone, and the woman standing in the midst." (v. 9) The law had never done this. They had learnt and trifled with the law up to this time; they had freely used it, as men do still, to convict other people. But here was the light of God shining full on their sinful condition, as well as on the law. It was the light of God that reserved all its rights to the law, but itself shone with such spiritual force as had never reached their consciences before, and drove out the faithless hearts which desired not the knowledge of God and His ways. And this a waif tossed haphazard on the broken coast of our gospel! Nay, brethren, your eyes are at fault; it is a ray of light from Christ, and shines just where it should.

It was not exactly, as Augustine says, "Relicti sunt duo, misera, et misericordia" (In Jo. Evang. Tr., xxxiii. 5); for here the Lord is acting as light. Therefore, instead of saying, thy sins are forgiven, He asks, "Woman, where are those thine accusers? hath no man condemned thee? She said, No man, Lord. And Jesus said unto her, neither do I condemn thee: go, and sin no more"[6]. It is not pardon, nor mercy, but light. "Go, and sin no more" (not, "Thy faith hath saved thee: go in peace"). Man invented such a story as this! Who since the world began, had he set to work to imagine an incident to illustrate the chapter, could or would have framed such an one as this? Where is there anything like it, that poet, philosopher, historian ever wrote, ever conceived? Produce the Protevangelion, the gospel of Nicodemus, or any other such early writing. These, indeed, are the genuine productions of man; but what a difference from that before us! Yet is it in the truest sense original, entirely distinct from any other fact, either in the Bible, or anywhere else, not, of course, excepting John himself. Nevertheless, its air, scope, and character can be proved, I think, to suit John, and no other; and this particular context in John,

---

[6] The fact that κατακρίνω is found here twice, and here only in John, is of no weight against the genuineness of the passage. It is the strict judicial term for passing an adverse sentence among men. How, where, could this be anywhere else in John? It is not true that κρίνω is ever used in this sense anywhere in John. It means, and should always be rendered, "judge," not "condemn," though the effect for the guilty (and man is guilty) be necessarily condemnation.

and no other. No theory is less reasonable than that this can be either a mere floating tradition stuck in here by some chance, or the work of a forger's mind. I do not think it harsh, but charitable to speak thus plainly; for the course of incredulity is now running strong' and Christians can hardly avoid hearing of these questions. I therefore do not refuse this opportunity of leading any simple souls to see how truly divine the whole bearing of this portion is — how exactly apposite to that which the Lord insists on throughout the chapter. For, immediately after, we have doctrine unfolded which, no doubt, goes farther, but is intimately connected, as no other chapter is, with the story[7].

---

[7] Among the detailed objections to the genuineness of the passage (John 7:53-8:11), it is contended that the evidence of Augustine and Nicon (who distinctly tell us that it was expunged wilfully on account of the supposed license it gave to sin) does not account for the omission of John 7:53. But this is short-sighted. For the going of each to his home is in evident connection with, and contra-distinction to, the going of Jesus to the mount of Olives. He was ever the stranger here. And what gospel, or whose style, does this simple but profound contrast suit so much as John? (Compare John 20:10, 11) We know, from John 18:2, that this neighbourhood was the frequent resort of Jesus with His disciples. Next, the idea of many distinct and independent texts (as distinguished from abundance of various readings) seems an evident exaggeration. Take the fact, that this is eked out by putting the Received Text as one; the text of D (or Beza's Cambridge Uncial) as another; and that of most of the MSS. E F G H K M S U, etc., as a third. Now, what right has the Received Text to be thus ranged? It was formed by collating some of those very manuscripts which are thrown together as a third text. The true conclusion, therefore, is simply the not at all unprecedented phenomenon that D differs considerably from almost if not all other manuscripts, and that the Received Text is but a poor approximation to a text based on a collation of manuscripts. A really standard text, which gives just but discriminating value to an worthy witnesses, is as yet a desideratum. Thirdly, what the contents of the passage are which countenances the notion that there is some inherent defect in the text to invalidate its claim to a place in the sacred narrative I cannot divine, as it is not here explained. The fourth objection is the very general concurrence of the MSS. that contain the passage in placing it here. Why this place, of all others, should have been

Jesus spoke again to them (the interrupters having disappeared). "I am the light of the world." He had just acted as light among those who had appealed to law; He here goes on, but widens the sphere. He says, "I am the light of the world." it is not merely dealing with scribes and Pharisees. Further, "He that followeth me shall not walk in darkness, but shall have the light of life." The life was the light of men, the perfect display and guide of the life He was to His followers. The law never is this — good if a man use it lawfully, but not for a righteous man whose Christ is. So Christ tells the Pharisees who objected that He knew whence He came, and whither He was going: they were in the dark, and knew nothing of it. They were in the unrelieved darkness of the

---

selected, will be no difficulty to those who feel with me; but, on the contrary, in my judgment, it refutes the "desperate resource" (as it is even allowed to be, strange to say, by those who adopt it), that the evangelist may have in this solitary case incorporated a portion of the current oral tradition into his narrative, which was afterwards variously corrected from the gospel to the Hebrews, or other traditional sources, and from different diction put in at the end of Luke 21, or elsewhere. I am convinced, that where there is a real understanding of John 8 as a whole, the opening incident will be felt to be a necessary exordium of fact before the discourse which, to my mind, manifestly and certainly grew out of it, as surely as it happened then, and at no other time. Lastly, the mind which could conceive that the fact, as well as the tone or the moral drift of this incident, fits in to the end of Luke 21 rather than to the beginning of John 8, seems so decidedly imaginative, that reasoning is here out of place, particularly as it is allowed, along with this, that its occurrence here (spite of the evidence of some cursive MSS. for Luke 21) seems much in its favour. Lastly, I have examined with care, and satisfied myself, that the alleged weightiest argument against the passage, in its entire diversity from the style of John's narrative, is superficial and misleading. Some peculiar words are required by the circumstance; and the general cast and character of the passage, so far from being alien to the evangelist's manner, seems to me, on the contrary, in his spirit, rather than in any other inspired writer's, no matter in — which of the manuscripts we read it. D is the copy which makes the chief inroads; this is a common thing with that venerable, but most faulty document.

world, they judged after the flesh. Not so Jesus: He did not judge. Yet, if He did, His judgment was true; for He was not alone, but His Father was with Him. And their law bid them bow to two witnesses. But what witnesses? His testimony was so decided, that the reason why they did not then lay hands on Him was simply this — His hour was not yet come. (Verses 12-20)

The Lord throughout the chapter speaks with more than usual solemnity, and with increasing plainness to His enemies, who knew neither Him nor His Father. They should die in their sins; and whither He went, they could not come. They were from beneath — of this world; He from above, and not of this world.

The truth is, that throughout the gospel He speaks as One consciously rejected, but morally judging all things as the Light. He therefore does not scruple to push things to an extremity, to draw out their real character and state most distinctly; to pronounce on them as from beneath, as He Himself from above; to show that there was no resemblance between them and Abraham, but rather Satan, and not the smallest communion in their thoughts with His Father's. Hence it is, too, that later on He lets them know that the time is coining when they should know who He was, but too late. He is the rejected light of God, and light of the world, from the first, and all through; but, more than this, He is the light of God, not only in deed, but in His word; as elsewhere He let them know they would be judged by it in the last day. Hence, when they asked Him who He was, He answers them to that effect; and I refer to it the more, because the force is imperfectly given, and even wrongly, in verse 25: "Who art thou? And Jesus saith unto them, Even the same that I said unto you from the beginning." Not only is there no need of adding "the same," but there is nothing that answers to "from the beginning." And this, again, has involved our translators in a change of tense, which is not merely uncalled for, but spoils the true idea. Our Lord does not refer to what He had said at or from any starting-point, but to what He speaks always, as then also. In every respect the sense of the Holy Ghost is enfeebled, changed, and even destroyed in the common version. What our Lord did answer is incomparably more forcible, and in exact accordance with the doctrine of the chapter, and the incident that begins it. They asked Him who He was. His answer is this: "Absolutely that which I also am speaking to you." I am thoroughly, essentially what I also speak. It is not only that He is the light, and that there is no darkness in Him — as there is none in God, so none in Him; but, as to the principle of His being, He is what He utters. And, indeed, of Him only is this true. A Christian may be said to be light in the Lord; but of none, save Jesus, could it be said, that the word he discourses is the expression of what he is. Jesus is the truth. Alas! we know that, so false is human nature and the world, nothing but the power of the Spirit, revealing Christ to us through the Word, keeps us even as believers from departure into error, misconduct, and evil of any kind. None but One could say, "I am what I speak." And this is precisely what Christ is showing throughout the scene. He was the light to convict the doers of darkness, however hidden; He was the light which made others — no matter what they might have been in the world — to be light, if they followed Himself, God manifest in flesh. He manifested God, and made man manifest also. Everything was manifested by the light. Who is He? "Absolutely (τὴν ἀρχὴν) what I speak." What He utters in speech is what He is. There was not the smallest deflection from the truth; His every word and way declared it. There was never the appearance of what He was not. He is always, and in every particular, what He speaks.

How entirely this falls in with what we have elsewhere, does not need to be pressed. We see farther on the same doctrine, only ever expanding; revelation clearer, and more antagonistic to more and more determined unbelief. He lets them know, that when they have lifted up the Son of man, then they shall know that Jesus is He (the truth would be thoroughly out), "and that I do nothing of myself; but as my Father hath taught me, I speak these things." It is not miracles here, but the truth. He not only is the truth in His own person, but He speaks it. He speaks it to the world also; for all through John's gospel, although it be the eternal life that was with the Father, the Word that was with God in the beginning, still, He is also (from John 1:14) a man on earth — a real, true man here below, however truly God. And so it is in this chapter. It began by showing that He is so in act; then it opens out that He is so in word. He said to the world what He heard from Him that sent Him — as they rightly understood, from the Father.

He pursues the same line in dealing with the Jews who believed in Him (verse 31): "If ye continue in my word, then are ye my disciples indeed; and ye shall know the truth, and the truth shall make you free. They answered him, we be Abraham's seed, and were never in bondage to any man: how sayest thou, Ye shall be made free? Jesus answered them, Verily, verily, I say unto you, whosoever committeth sin is the servant of sin. And the servant abideth not in the house for ever: but the Son abideth ever. If the Son therefore shall make you free, ye shall be free indeed." Thus His word (not the law) is the sole means of knowing the truth and its liberty. It was not merely a question of commands, or of something God wanted from man. That had been given, and tried; and what was the end of it for them and Him? Now much more was at stake, even the manifestation of God in Christ to the world, and this also in His word, in the truth. It became a test, therefore, of the truth; and if they continued in His word, they should be His disciples indeed; and should know the truth, and the truth should make them free.

But then there is another thing required to set free, or rather which does à fortiori set free. The truth learnt in the word of Jesus is the only foundation. But if received, it is not merely that I have the truth, so to speak, as an expression of His mind, but of Himself — of His person. Hence it is that He touches on this point in verse 36: "If the Son therefore shall make you free, ye shall be free indeed." It is not merely, then, the truth making free, but the Son. He who pretends to receive the truth, but does not bow before the glory of the Son, proves that there is no truth in him. He that receives the truth might at first be very ignorant; the truth may be, then, nothing more than that which lets in the light of God graciously, but in a limited measure. It is rarely that all at once the full glory of Christ bursts in upon the soul. As with the disciples, so it might be with any soul now. There might be real, but gradual perception; but the truth invariably works thus, where God is the teacher. Then, as light increases, and the glory of Christ shines more distinctly, the heart welcomes Him; and so much the more rejoices as He is exalted. On the contrary, where it is not the truth, but theory or tradition — a mere reasoning or sentiment about Christ, the heart is offended by the full presentation of His glory, stumbles at it, and turns away from Him, just because it cannot bear the strength and brightness of that divine fulness which was in Christ: it knows not God, nor Jesus Christ whom He has sent. Eternal life is unknown and unenjoyed.

Further, the Lord brings out here another thing worthy of all attention; especially as the same principle runs through from the incident at the beginning of the chapter. It is not merely light, truth, and the Son known in the person of Christ, but also as contrasted with the law. Did they boast in the law? What place had they under it? Slaves! Yes, and they were faithless to it; they broke the law; they were slaves of sin. It is not the slave, but the Son, who abides in the house. Thus the law is not in any way lowered, but at the same time there is the bright contrast of Christ with it. The law has its just place; it is for servants, and deals with them justly. The consequence is, there is no permanence for them, any more than liberty. Law could not meet the case; nothing, and none short of the Son. "Whosoever committeth sin is the servant of sin." Was not this precisely what He had brought home to the conscience at the beginning of the chapter? Before God (and He was God) it was not what the poor woman had done that was all, but what they were, and they were convicted of sin; they were not without sin. He had said, "The servant abideth not in the house;" and this was precisely the case with them; they were obliged to go[8]. "But the Son abideth ever," and so He does in the best, and highest, and truest estate. Thus the doctrine entirely harmonizes with the fact, and in a way that does not appear at first sight, but only as we look into it a little more closely, and search into the depths of the living word of God, though none of us can boast of the progress we have made. Nevertheless, we may be permitted to say, that the more closely we are given of God to apprehend the truth, the more the divine perfectness of the entire picture becomes manifest to our souls.

I need not go through the particulars which the Lord brings out in laying bare the condition of the Jews, the seed (not the children) of Abraham, but really of their father the devil, and manifesting it in the two characters of liar and murderer. They did not know His speech, because they could not hear His word. The truth meant is the key to the outer vehicle of it — just the reverse of man's knowledge. In fine, all is shown in its true essential character here, the convicted one and her accusers, the Jews, the world, the disciples, the truth, the Son, Satan himself, God Himself. Not only is Abraham[9] seen truly (not as misrepresented in his seed), but One who was greater than "our father" Abraham, who would say, If I honour myself, my honour is nothing; but who could say (with a verily, verily), "BEFORE ABRAHAM WAS, I AM." He is the light in deed and word. He says so. Then He deals with them, convicting them more and more. He shows that the truth is found here only in His word. He, the

---

[8] "They were struck by the power of the word of Christ," says an opponent of the claim of the commencing section to a genuine and divinely given place in the chapter, unconscious that he is thereby illustrating its connection with the whole current of the chapter.

[9] I apprehend that by "my day" He means the day of Christ's glory; not vaguely the time of Christ, but the day when He will be displayed in glory. "Your father Abraham rejoiced to see my day." He looked for that day of Christ's appearing in glory, and he "saw it, and was glad." It was the day when the promises would be accomplished, and very naturally he who had the promises looked for the time when they are to be made good in Christ.

witness, testifies that He is the Son. But the chapter does not end before He announces His eternal Godhead. He is God Himself, yet hides Himself when they took up stones to stone Him. His hour was not yet come. This is the truth of them, as of Him. He was God. Such is the truth. Short of this, we have not the truth of Christ. But it is the growing rejection of Christ's word that leads Him on step by step to the assertion that He was very God, though a man upon the earth.

Like the preceding, John 9 shows us the Lord rejected — here in His work, as there in His word. The difference a little answers to what we have seen in John 5, 6. In the fifth chapter He is the quickening Son of God; but all testimonies are vain, and judgment awaits the unbeliever — a resurrection of judgment. In John 6. He is seen as the suffering Son of man, who takes the place of humiliation, instead of the kingdom which they wanted to force on Him. But no; this was not the purpose for which He had come, though true in its own time; but what He took, and took because His eye was ever single, viewed as man, was for God's glory, not for His own; and the real glory of God in a ruined world is only met by the service and death of the Son of man dying for sinners and for sin. Somewhat similarly in John 8 He is the rejected Word, who confesses Himself (when most scorned and men are ready to stone Him) to be the everlasting God Himself. As man becomes more hardened in unbelief, Christ becomes more pointed and plain in the assertion of the truth. Thus the more it is pressed down, the more the brightness of the truth makes its way out, that He is God. They had fully heard now who He was, and therefore must He be ignominiously cast out. His words brought God too close, too really; and they would not bear them.

But now He is rejected in another way, and in this it is as man, though declaring Himself and worshipped as Son of God. We shall see that there is stress on His manhood, more especially as the necessary mould or form which divine grace took to effect the blessing of man, to work the works of God in grace on the earth. Accordingly, here it is not merely that man is seen to be guilty, but blind from his birth. Doubtless there is light that discovers man in his evil and. unbelief; but man is sought and met by His grace; for here the man had no thought of being healed — never asked Jesus to heal him. There was no cry here to the Son of David. This we hear most properly in the other gospels, which develop the last offer of the Messiah to the Jews. In every one of the gospels, indeed, we have Him finally presented as the Son of David; and therefore, although it be the proper province of Matthew, yet inasmuch as all the synoptic gospels dwell on our Lord at the close as Son of David, all the gospels give the story of the blind man at Jericho. Matthew, however, gives blind men over and over again, crying to Him, "Son of David." The reason is, I suppose, that not merely is He so presented at the last, but all through in Matthew. In John this case does not appear at all; no blind man cries to the Son of David throughout. What is brought before us in the man, blind from his birth, is a wholly different truth. It was, indeed, the most desperate case. Instead of the man looking to Christ, it is Christ that looks at the man, without a single cry or appeal to Him. It is absolute grace. If it be not the Father seeking, at any rate it is the Son. It is One who had deigned to become man in love to man. He is seeking, though rejected, to display the grace of God toward this poor blind beggar in his abject need: "As Jesus passed by, he saw a man which was blind from his birth. And his disciples asked him, saying, Master, who did sin, this man, or his parents, that he was born blind?"

They had nothing better than Jewish thoughts about the case. But all through the gospel of John Christ is setting aside these thoughts on every side, whether in enquirers outside, or more particularly in disciples, who were under this pernicious influence like other people. Here the Lord answered, "Neither hath this man sinned, nor his parents." The ways of God are not as man's; and their revelation stands in contrast with Jewish notions of retributive justice. The reason lay deeper than what his parents deserved, or the foresight of what he would do amiss. Not that the man and his parents were not sinners; but the eye of Jesus saw beyond nature, or law, or government, in the man's blindness from his birth. To divine goodness, the inner and true and ultimate reason, God's reason — if one may be permitted such a phrase — was to furnish an opportunity for Christ to work the works of God on the earth. How blessedly grace operates in, and judges of, a hopeless case! That it was wholly outside the resources of man made it just the occasion for Jesus, for the works of God. This is the point of the chapter — Jesus working the works of God in free unconditional grace. In John 8 the prominent feature. is the word of God; here, the works of God made effectual and manifest in grace. "I must work the works of him that sent me while it is day." Therefore, can one say, that it is unqualified grace, because it is not merely God mercifully answering man's appeal, and blessing man's work, but God sending, and Christ working. "I must work the works of him that sent me." What grace (save in Jesus all through) can be compared with this? Jesus, then, was doing this work "while it is day." Day was while He was present with them. Night was coming, which would be, for the Jew, the personal absence of the Messiah; indeed, such for any would be the departure of the Son of God. "The night cometh when no man can work." (Verse 4) Higher things might follow in their season, and brighter light suited to them when the day should dawn, and the day-star arise in hearts established with grace. But here it is the time of the absence of Jesus in contrast with His presence on earth as He then was. "As long as I am in the world, I am the light of the world." (Verse 5)

This establishes very plainly the fact, that these two chapters are so far linked together, in that they look at Christ as light, and the light of the world too. But, far from being confined to Israel, it rather sets aside the Jewish system, which assumes to order things justly now according to man's conduct, thus ignoring man's ruin by sin, and God's grace in Christ as the sole deliverance. Here it is not so much the light by the word convicting man, and bringing out God's nature and the reality of

His own personal glory, but "the light of the world" as manifesting God graciously working in power contrary to nature. It was a question not of light for eyes, but of giving power to see the light to one wholly and evidently incapable of seeing as he was. Hence we do well to remark the peculiarity in the Lord's manner of working. He lays clay upon the man's eyes; an extraordinary step at first sight. In truth, it was the shadow of Himself become man, an apt figure of the human body which He took in order therein to do God's will. He was not simply Son of God, but Son of God possessed of a body prepared of God. (Heb. 10) He became man; and yet the fact of the body of Christ — of God's Son being found in fashion as a man — only and greatly increases the difficulty at first sight, because nobody, apart from the word of God, would look for a divine person in such a guise. But when faith bows to the word, and accepts the will of God in it, how precious the grace, how wise the ordering yea, how indispensable it is learnt to be! So with the man already blind before. Putting the plaster of clay over his eyes did not at once mend his blindness in the least; but, if anything, the contrary — would have hindered his seeing, had he seen before. But when he goes at the word of Jesus, and washes in the pool of Siloam — that is, when the word is applied in the Holy Ghost to his case, revealing Jesus as the sent One of God (compare John 5:24), all was so far plain. It was not a mere man who had spoken; he apprehended in Jesus One Sent (for the pool to which the Lord directed the man to wash his clay-covered eyes in was called "Siloam;" that is, it bore the very name of "sent"). It was then understood that Jesus had a mission on earth to work the works of God. Though, of course, man born of a woman, He was more than human: He was the Sent One — the Sent of the Father in love into this world, to work effectually where man was entirely incapable even of helping in any way.

Thus the truth was in process of application, so to speak. The man goes his way, washes, and comes seeing. The word of God explains this mystery. The Son's taking humanity is ever a blinding fact to nature; but he who is not disobedient to the word will assuredly not fail to find in the acknowledgment of the truth Christ's glory under His manhood, as well as the need of his own soul met with a power and promptness which answers, as it is due, to His glory who wrought in grace here below.

Nevertheless, the word of the Lord tried him as ever; other hearts were tested by it too. The neighbours were astonished, and questions arise; the Pharisees are stirred but divided (for this miracle, also, was wrought on a sabbath). The parents being summoned, as well as himself questioned, all stand to the great and indisputable fact: the man just healed was their child, and he had been born blind. The man indeed witnessed what he believed of Jesus, and the threat of the consequences was only made the clearer, even though there was a total avoidance of all dangerous answers on the parents' part, and a determination to reject Christ and those who confessed Him in the Pharisees. The work of grace was hated, and especially because it was wrought on the sabbath day. For this bore solemn witness, that in the truth of things before God there was no sabbath possible for them: He must work if man was to be delivered and blessed. Of course, there was the holy form, and there was no doubt as to the duty; but if God revealed Himself on earth, neither forms nor duties, paid after a sort by sinful men, could hide the awful reality that man was incapable of keeping such a sabbath as God could recognise. The day had been sanctified from the beginning; the duty of the Jew was unquestionable; but sin was man's state; — after every remedial measure, he was thoroughly and only evil continually.

In fact, so far the Jew quite understood, as far as that went, the moral meaning of the Lord's working thus both either on the impotent man before, and now on the blind man. For such deeds on the sabbath did pronounce sentence of death on that whole system, and on the great badge of relationship between God and Israel. If Jesus was true God as well as man, if He was really the light of the world, yet wrought on the sabbath day, there was plain evidence on God's part of what He thought of Israel. They felt it to be a matter of life and death. But the man was led on by these conscienceless attacks, as is always the case where there is simple faith. The effort to destroy the person of Christ and to undermine His glory only developed, in the goodness of God, that divine work which had already touched his soul, as well as given him eyes to see. Thus was his faith exercised and cleared, side by side with the unbelief and hostility of the enemies of Christ. The consequence is, that we have a beautiful history in this chapter of the man led on step by step; first owning the work the Lord had wrought with simplicity, and therefore in force of truth: what he does not know he owned with just the same frankness. Then, when the Pharisees were divided, and he was appealed to once more, "He is a prophet" was his distinct answer. Then, when the fact was only the more established by the parents, spite of their timidity, the hypocritical effort to honour God at the expense of Jesus draws out the most withering refutation (not without a taunt) from him who had been blind. (Verses 24-33) This closed, they could not answer, and cast him out. (Verse 34)

How beautiful to mark the Spirit's love, dwelling fully and minutely on a blind beggar taught of God, thus gradually and evermore beating their in credulous objections smaller than when they cast him out as dirt in the streets! What a living picture of the new witness for Christ! A character plain, honest, energetic, not always the most gracious, but certainly confronted with the most heartless and false of adversaries. But if the man finds himself out of the synagogue, he is soon in the presence of Christ. The religious world of that day could not endure a witness of divine power and grace which they themselves, feeling not the need, denied, denounced, and did all they could to destroy. Outside them, but with Jesus, he learns more deeply than ever, so as to fill his soul with profound joy and gladness, that the wondrous healer of his blindness was not merely a prophet, but the Son of God — just object of faith and worship. Thus clearly we have in this case the rejection of Jesus viewed, not in open attack on His own person, as in the. chapter before, where they took up stones to stone Him, but here rather in His friends, whom He had first met in sovereign grace, and did not let them go till fully blessed, ending in Jesus worshipped outside the synagogue as the Son of God. (Verses 38-40)

Then the Lord declares the issues of His coming. "For judgment," He says, "I am come into this world, that they which see not might see; and that they which see might be made blind." In this gospel He lad said before, that it was to save and give life, not to judge, that He came. Such was the aim of His heart, at all cost to Himself; but the effect was moral in one way or the other, and this now. Manifest judgment awaits the evil by-and-by. And some of the Pharisees which were with him heard these words, and said unto him, are we blind also? Jesus said unto them, if ye were blind, ye should have no sin: but now ye say, we see; therefore, your sin remaineth." They were offended at the notion of their not seeing. Did they insist that they saw? The Lord admits the plea. If they felt their sin and shortcoming, there might be a hope. As it was, then, sin remained. The boast, like the excuse, of unbelief is invariably the ground of divine judgment.

John 10 pursues the subject and opens out into a development, not of the spiritual history of a sheep of Christ, but of the Shepherd Himself, from first to last, here below. Hence, the Lord does not rest in a judgment extorted by their unbelief, and in contrast with the deliverance of faith, but develops the ways of grace here, as always in marked antithesis with the Jewish system, though connected with the man for His sake turned out of the synagogue, then found by Himself, and led into the fullest perception of His own glory outside the Jews, where alone real worship is possible. Accordingly, our Lord traces this new history — His own from the beginning.

"Verily, verily, I say unto you, He that entereth not by the door into the sheepfold, but climbeth up some other way, the same is a thief and a robber." It was not so with Jesus. He had entered in by the door, according to every requisition of the Scriptures.

Although Son, He had submitted to each ordinance which God had laid down for the Shepherd of His earthly people. He accomplished the work that God had marked out for Him in prophecy and type. What had been required or stipulated, according to the law, that had He not rendered in full tale? He was born at the measured time, in the due place, from the sworn stock, and of the defined mother, according to the written word. God had taken care beforehand to make each important point plain, by which the true Christ of God was to be recognised; and all had been fulfilled thus far in Jesus — thus far; for it is quite allowed that all the prophecies of subjugation and judgment, with the reign over the earth, remain to be accomplished. "To him," He says, "the porter openeth." This had been realized. Witness the Holy Ghost's action in Simeon and Anna, not to speak of the mass; and, above all, in John the Baptist. God had wrought by His grace in Israel, and there were godly hearts prepared for Him there.

"And the sheep hear his voice." (Verse 3) So we find in the gospels, particularly Luke's, from the beginning. And he calleth his own sheep by name, and leadeth them out" — an evident allusion to what had befallen the blind man. No doubt he had been turned out of the synagogue; but Christ imprints, on this, their wicked act, His own interpretation, according to divine counsels. Little did the man know at that painful moment, that it was in reality grace which was leading him out. If it was a little before His own public and final rejection, it was, after all, the same principle at the bottom. The disciple is not above his master; but every one that is perfect shall be as his master. "He goeth before them." This seems to refer to the manner in which it had been, and should be, accomplished. Already had the Lord tasted the enmity and scorn of man, and especially of the Jews; but He also knew the depths of shame and suffering which He must soon pass through, before there was an open separation of the sheep. Thus, whether it were done virtually or formally, in either case Jesus went before, and the sheep followed; "for they know his voice." This is their spiritual instinct, as it is their security — not skill in determining or refuting error, but simple cleaving to Christ and the truth. See this exemplified in the once blind man. What weight had the Pharisees with his conscience? None whatever. They, on the contrary, felt he taught them. "A stranger will they not follow," any more than he would follow the Pharisees. For now, by the new eyes which the Lord had given him, he could discern their vain pretensions, and their hostility against Jesus so much the worse, because coupled with "Give God the praise." "A stranger will they not follow, but will flee from him" — not because they are learned in the injurious jargon of strangers, "for they know not the voice of strangers." They know the Shepherd's voice, and this they follow. It is the love of what is good, and not skill in finding out what is evil. Some may have power to sift and discern the unsound; but this is not the true, direct, divine means of safety for the sheep of Christ. There is a much more real, immediate, and sure way. It is simply this: they cannot rest without the voice of Christ; and that which is not the voice of Christ they do not follow. What more suitable to them, or more worthy of Him?

As these things were not understood, the Lord opens out the truth still more plainly in what follows. Here (verse 7) He begins by taking the place of "the door of the sheep;" not, be it observed, of the sheepfold, but of the sheep. He had entered in Himself by the door, not of the sheep, of course, but by the door into the sheepfold. He entered in according to each sign and token — moral, miraculous, prophetic, or personal — which God had given to His ancient people to know Him by. But enter as He might, the people who broke the law refused the Shepherd; and the end of it was, that He leads His own sheep outside, Himself going before them. Now, there is more, and He says, "I am the door of the sheep." The contrast of pretended or merely human shepherds is given in the next verse, which is parenthetical. "All that ever came before me [such as Theudas and Judas] are thieves and robbers [they secretly or openly enriched themselves by the sheep]: but the sheep did not hear them."

In verse 9 He enlarges. "I am the door: by me if any man enter in, he shall be saved, and shall go in and out, and find pasture." The portion He gives the sheep is a contrast with the law in another way; not as light simply, as in the beginning of John 8, in detecting all sin and every sinner. Now, it is grace in its fulness. "By me," He says — not by circumcision, or the law — "By me if any man enter in." There was no question of entering in by the law; for it dealt with those who were already in a recognised relation with God. But now there is an invitation to those without. "By me if any man enter in, he shall be saved." Salvation is the first need of a sinner, and certainly the Gentile needs it as much as the Jew. "By me if any man" — no matter who he may be, if he enter, he shall be saved. Nevertheless, it is only for those that enter in. There is no salvation for such as abide outside Christ. But this is not all; for grace with Christ freely gives, not salvation alone, but all things. Even now, too, "he shall go in and out." It is not only that there is life and salvation in Christ, but there is liberty, in contrast with the law. "And he shall find pasture." Besides, there is food assured. Thus we have here an ample provision for the sheep. To him that enters by Christ there is salvation, there is liberty, there is food.

Again, the Lord contrasts others with Himself. The thief cometh not, but for to steal, and to kill, and to destroy." By their fruits they should know them. How could the sheep trust such shepherds as these? "I am come that they might have life, and that they might have it more abundantly." There had been life when there was only a promise; there had been life all through the dealings of law. Clearly Christ had ever been the means of life from the day death entered the world. But now He was come, it was not only that they might have life, but that they might have it "more abundantly." This was the effect of the presence of God's Son in this world. Was it not right and becoming, that when the Son of God did humble Himself in this world, even to death, the death of the cross, dying also in atonement for sinners, God should mark this infinite fact and work and person by an incomparably richer blessing than ever had been diffused before? I cannot conceive it otherwise than the Word shows it is, consistently with the glory of God, even the Father.

Further, He was not only the door of the sheep, and then the door for others to enter in, but He says (verse 11), "I am the good shepherd: the good shepherd giveth his life for the sheep." It is no longer only in contrast with a thief or a robber, with murderous intent or evidently selfish purposes of the worst kind, but there might be others characterised by a milder form of human iniquity — not destroyers of the sheep, but self-seeking men. "He that. is an hireling, and not the shepherd, whose own the sheep are not, seeth the wolf coming, and leaveth the sheep, and fleeth: and the wolf catcheth them, and scattereth the sheep. The hireling fleeth, because he is an hireling, and careth not for the sheep." Christ, as the good shepherd, does nothing of the kind, but remains to suffer all for them, instead of running away when the wolf came. "I am the good shepherd, and know those that are mine, and am known by mine, as the Father knoweth me, and I know the Father." Such is the true sense of the verse. The 14th and 15th verses really form one sentence. They are not divided as we have them in our Bibles. The meaning is, that He showed Himself as the good Shepherd because He knew the sheep, and was known of them, just. as He knew the Father, and was known of the Father. The mutuality of knowledge between the Father and the Son is the pattern of the knowledge between the Shepherd and the sheep. In what a wondrous. place this puts us and the character of knowledge we possess. The knowledge which grace gives to the sheep is so truly divine that the Lord has nothing to compare it with, except the knowledge that exists between the Father and the Son. Nor is it merely a question of knowledge, intimate and perfect and divine as it is; but, moreover, "I lay down my life for the sheep." Other sheep, too, He intimates here, He had, who were to be brought in, that did not belong to the Jewish fold; He clearly looks out into the world, as always in the gospel of John. There was to be one flock (not fold), one Shepherd.

Moreover, in order to open yet more the ineffable complacency of the Father in His work abstractedly, He adds, "Therefore doth my Father love me, because I lay down my life." Not here "for the sheep," but simply, "that I might take it again." (Verse 17) That is to say, besides laying down His life for the sheep, He laid down His life to prove His perfect confidence in His Father. Impossible for another, or all others, to give so much. Even He could not give more than His life. Any other thing would not be comparable to the laying down of His life. It was the most complete, absolute giving up of Himself; and He did give up Himself, not merely for the gracious end of winning the sheep to God from the spoiler, but with the still more blessed and glorious aim of manifesting, in a world where man had from the first dishonoured God, His own perfect confidence in His Father, and this as man. He laid it down that He might take it again. Thus, instead of continuing His life in dependence on His Father, He gives it up out of a still profounder and truly absolute dependence. "Therefore," says He, "doth my Father love me." This becomes a positive ground for the Father to love Him, additional to the perfection which had ever been seen in Him all His pathway through. Even more than this; although it is so expressly an act of His own, another astonishing principle is seen — the union of absolute devotedness on His own part, in perfect freeness of His will, with obedience. (Verse 18) Thus the very same act may be, and is (as we find it in all its perfection in Christ) His own will, and yet along with this simple submission to His Father's commandment. In truth, He and the Father were one; and so He does not stop till we have this fully expressed in verse 30. He and His Father were one — one in everything; not only in love and gracious counsel for the sheep, but in nature, too — in that divine nature which, of course, was the ground of all the grace.

But, besides this, the unbelief of the Jews brings out another thing; that is, the perfect security of the sheep — a very important question, because He was going to die. His death is in view: what will the sheep do then? Would the death of Christ in any way imperil the sheep? The very reverse. The Lord declares this in a most distinct manner. He says, "My sheep hear my voice, and I know them, and they follow me: and I give unto them eternal life; and they shall never perish, neither shall any man pluck them out of my hand." (Verses 27, 28) First of all, the life is everlasting. But then it is not merely that the thing itself is eternal, but they shall never perish; for it might be pretended, that though the life lasts for ever, this is conditional on something in its recipients. Nay, "they shall never perish" — the sheep themselves. Thus, not merely the life, but those who have it by grace in Christ, shall never perish. To conclude and crown all, as far as their security was concerned, the question is answered as to any hostile power. What about some one external to them? Nay; there again, as there was no internal source of weakness that could jeopard the life, so there should be no external power to cause anxiety. If there was any power that might do so righteously, surely it must be God's own; but, contrariwise, they were in the Father's hand, no less than in the Son's hand — none could pluck them out. Thus the Lord fenced them round even by His death, as well as by that eternal life which was in Him, the superiority of which over death was proved by His authority to take it again in resurrection. This was the life more abundantly which they derived from Him. Why should any one wonder at its power? He was, for the sheep, against all adversaries; and so was the Father. Yea, "I and the Father are one." (Verses 29, 30)

As there had been a division among the Jews for His sayings, and their appeal in doubt to Him had drawn out both His treatment of them as unbelievers, and the security of the sheep who heeded His voice and followed Him, as He knew them (ver. 19-30) so our Lord, in the presence of their hatred and still growing enmity (ver. 31), convicts them of the futility of their objection on their own ground. Did they find fault because He took the place of being the Son of God? Yet they must allow that kings, governors, judges, according to their law, were called gods. "If he called them gods, unto whom the word of God came, and the scripture cannot be broken; say ye of him, whom the Father hath sanctified, and sent into the world, thou blasphemest; because I said, I am the Son of God?" A fortiori had He not a place which no king ever had? Did He, on their own principles, blaspheme then, because He said He was the Son of God? But He goes far beyond this. If they regarded not God's word, nor His words, He appeals to His works. "If I do not the works of my Father, believe me not. But if I do, though ye believe not me, believe the works: that ye may know, and believe, that the Father is in me, and I in him." This connects, as I apprehend, the tenth chapter with the foregoing, and is in contrast with the eighth. They had thus repeatedly sought to kill Him, and He abandons them for the place in which John first baptized. In the face of total rejection, and in every point of view, both as the expression of God in the world, and of His working the works of grace in the world, the result was plain. Man, the Jew especially, settles down in resolute unbelief and deadly hostility; but, on the other hand, the indefeasible security of the sheep, the objects of grace, only comes out with so much the greater clearness and decision.

Nevertheless, though all was really closed, God would manifest by a full and final testimony what was the glory of Christ, rejected as He was, and previous to His death. And accordingly, in John 11 and 12 is given a strikingly rich presentation of the Lord Jesus, in many respects entirely differing from all the others; for while it embraces what is found in the synoptists (that is, the accomplishment of prophecy in His offer of Himself to Zion as the Son of David), John brings in a fulness of personal glory that is peculiar to his gospel.

Here we begin with that which John alone records — the resurrection of Lazarus. Some have wondered that it appears only in the latest gospel; but it is given there for a very simple and conclusive reason. The resurrection of Lazarus was the most distinct testimony possible, near Jerusalem, in the face of open Jewish enmity. It was the grandest demonstrative proof that He was the Son of God, determined to be the Son of God with power, according to the Spirit of holiness, by the resurrection from the dead. Who but He on earth could say, I am the resurrection and the life? Who had ever looked for more in Messiah Himself than Martha did — raising up the dead at the last day?

Here I may just observe, that Romans 1:4 does not restrict the meaning to the fact that He was determined to be the Son of God with power by His own resurrection. This is not what the verse states, but that resurrection of the dead, or the raising of dead persons, was the great proof that defined Him to be the Son of God with power. No doubt His own resurrection was the most astonishing instance of it; but His raising of dead persons in His ministry was a witness also, as the resurrection of His saints by-and-by will be the display of it. Hence the verse in Romans 1 expresses the truth in all its extent, and without specifying any one in particular. So Lazarus, as being the most conspicuous case of resurrection any where appearing in the gospels, except Christ's own, which all give, was the fullest testimony that even John rendered to that great truth. Hence, then, as one might expect from its character, the account is given with remarkable development in that gospel which is devoted to the personal glory of Jesus as the Son of God. To this attaches the revelation of the resurrection, and the life in Him as a, present thing, superior to all questions of prophetic time, or dispensations. It could be found nowhere else so appropriately as in John. The difficulty, therefore, in its occurrence here and not elsewhere, is really none whatever to any one who believes the object of God as apparent in the gospels themselves.

But, then, there is another feature that meets us in the story. Christ was not only the Son of God, but the Son of man. He was the Son of God, and a perfect man, in absolute dependence on His Father. He was not to be acted upon by any feeling, except the will of God. Thus He carries His divine sonship into His position as a man on earth, and He never allows that the glory of His person should in the smallest degree interfere with the completeness of His dependence and obedience. Hence, when the Lord hears the call, "Behold, he whom thou lovest is sick" —

the strongest possible appeal to the heart for acting at once on it — He does not go. His answer is most calm, and, if God be not before us, to mere human feeling it might seem indifferent. It was not so, but was utter perfection. "This sickness," He says, "is not unto death." Events might seem to contradict this; appearances might say it was to death, but Jesus was and is the truth always. "This sickness is not unto death, but for the glory of God, that the Son of God might be glorified thereby." And so it was. "Now, Jesus loved Martha, and her sister, and Lazarus." Whatever, therefore, it might appear, His affection was unquestionable. But, then, there are other and even deeper principles. His love for Mary, for Martha, and for Lazarus weakened in no respect His dependence on God; He waited on His Father's direction. So, "when he heard that he was sick, he abode two days still in the same place where he was. Then after that saith he to his disciples, let us go into Judea again. They say, Master, the Jews of late sought to stone thee; and goest thou thither again? Jesus answered, Are there not twelve hours in the day? If any man walk in the day he stumbleth not, because he seeth the light of this world. But if a man walk in the night he stumbleth, because there is no light in him." In Jesus there was nothing but perfect light. He was Himself the light. He walked in the sunshine of God. He was the very perfection of that which is only partially true with us in practice. "If, then, thine eye be single, thy whole body shall be full of light." Indeed, He was the light, as well as full of it. Walking accordingly in this world, He waited for the word of His Father. At once, when this came, He says, "Our friend Lazarus sleepeth, but I go that I may awake him out of sleep." There was no darkness in Him. All is plain, and He go" forth promptly with the knowledge of all He is going to do.

Then we have the ignorant thoughts of the disciples, though not unmixed with devotedness to His person. Thomas proposes that they should go to die with him. How marvellous is the unbelief even of the saints of God! He was going really to raise the dead; their only thought was to go and die with him. Such was a disciple's sombre anticipation. Our Lord does not say a word about it at the moment, but calmly leaves the truth to correct the error in due time. Then we have the wonderful interview with the sisters; and, finally, our Lord is at the grave, a consciously divine person, the Son of the Father, but in the perfectness of manhood, yet with such deep feeling as Deity alone could produce — not only sympathy with sorrow, but, above all, the sense of what death is in this world. Indeed, our Lord did not raise up Lazarus from the dead, until His own spirit had just as thoroughly taken, as it were, the sense of death on His soul, as when, in the removal of any sickness, He habitually felt its burden (Matt. 8); not, of course, in a low, literal, physical manner, but weighing it all in His spirit with His Father. Of us it is said, "with groanings that cannot be uttered." If Christ groaned, His could not but be a groan in accordance with the Spirit — justly and perfectly uttering the real fulness of the grief that His heart felt. In our case this could not be, because there is that which mars the perfectness of what is felt by us; but in the case of Christ, the Holy Ghost takes up and groans out that which we cannot fully express. Even in us He gives the sorrow a divine expression to God; and, of course, in Christ there was no shortcoming, no mingling of the flesh, but all was absolutely perfect. Hence, along with this, there comes the full answer of God to the divine glory and perfection of Christ. Lazarus comes forth at the word of Christ.

This seems to me of deep interest; for we are too apt to look on Christ merely as One whose power dealt with sickness and with the grave. But does it not weaken His power if the Lord Jesus Christ enters into the reality of the case before God? On the contrary, it better manifests the perfectness of His love, and the strength of His sympathy, to trace intelligently the way in which His spirit took up the reality of the ruin here below to bear and spread it before God. And I believe that this was true of everything in Christ. So it was before and when He came to the cross. Our Lord did not go there without feeling the past and present and future: the atoning work is not the same as the anguish of being cast off by His people, and the utter weakness of the disciples. Then the sense of what was coming was realized by His spirit before the actual fact. It is not true, but positively and wholly false doctrine, to confine our Lord Jesus to the matter of bearing our sin, though this was confessedly the deepest act of all. Of course, the atonement was only on the cross: the bearing of the wrath of God, when Christ was made sin, was exclusively then and there. But to find fault with the statement that Christ did in His own spirit realize beforehand what He was going to suffer on the cross, is to overlook much of His sufferings, to ignore truth, and despise Scripture — either leaving out a large portion of what God records about it, or confounding it with the actual fact, and only a part of it after all.

It is true that many Christians have been absorbed with the bare exertion of power in the miracles of Christ. In His healing of disease they have passed by the truth expressed in Isaiah 53:4, which Matthew applies to His life, and to which I have referred more than once. It seems undeniable, that not only was the power of God exhibited in those miracles, but that they afforded opportunity for the depth of His feelings to display itself, who had before Him the creature as God made it, and the deplorable havoc sin had wrought. Thus Jesus did perfectly what saints do with a mixture of human infirmity. Take again the fact that the Lord is pleased at times to put us through some exercise of heart before the actual trial comes: what is the effect of this? Do we bear the trial less because the soul has already felt it with God? Surely not. On the contrary, this is just what proves the measure of our spirituality; and the more we go through the matter with God, the power and blessing are so much the greater; so that when the trial comes, it might appear to an outside observer as if all was perfect calmness, and so indeed it is, or should be; and this because all has been out between ourselves and God. This, I admit, increases the pain of the trial immensely; but is this a loss? especially as at the same time there is strength vouchsafed to bear it. Thus the principle applies even to our little trials.

But Christ endured and did everything in perfection. Hence, even before Lazarus was raised up at the grave, we do not see or hear of One coming with divine power and majesty, and doing the miracle, if I may so say, off-hand. What can be more opposed to the truth? He who has such a meagre notion of the scene has everything to learn about it. Not that there was the smallest lack of consciousness of His glory; He is the Son of God unmistakably; He knows that His Father hears Him always; but none of these things hindered the Lord from groans and tears at the grave which was about to witness His power. None of them hindered the Lord from taking on His spirit the sense of death as no one else did. This is described by the Holy Ghost in the most emphatic language. "He groaned in spirit, and was troubled." But what was all this, compared with what. was soon to befall Himself when God entered into judgment with Him for our sins? It is not only granted, but insisted, that the actual expiation of sin, under divine wrath, was entirely and exclusively on the cross; but thence to assume that He did not previously go through with God the coming scene, and what was leading on to it, and everything that could add to the anguish of our Lord, is defective and erroneous teaching, however freely it is allowed that there was in the scene itself the endurance of wrath for sin which separates that hour from all that ever was or can be again.

Then, before the end of the chapter, the effect of all this divine testimony is shown. Man decides that the Lord must die; their intolerance of Jesus becomes now more pronounced. It was well known before. The giddy multitude may never have realised it till it came; but the religious folk, and the leaders at Jerusalem, had made up their minds about it long before. He must die. And now he who was high priest takes up the word, and gives — though a wicked man, yet not without the Spirit acting — the authoritative sentence about it which is recorded in our chapter. The resurrection power of the Son of God brought to a head the enmity of him who had the power of death. Jesus might have done such works at Nain or elsewhere, but to display them publicly at Jerusalem was an affront to Satan and his earthly instruments. Now that the glory of the Lord Jesus shone out so brightly, threatening the dominion of the prince of this world, there was no longer a concealment of the resolution taken by the religious world — Jesus must die.

In John 12, accordingly, we have this, the under-current, still, but in a beautiful contrast. The Spirit of God here works in grace touching the death of Jesus, just as much as Satan was goading on his children to hatred and murder. God knows how to guide a beloved one of His where Jesus was abiding for a little season before He suffered. It was Mary; for John lets us hear the Lord Jesus calling His own sheep by name; and however rightly Matthew and Mark do not disclose it, it was not consistent with John's view of the Lord that she should be called merely "a woman," In his gospel such touches come out distinctly; and so we have Mary, and Mary's act with greater fulness as to its great principles, than anywhere else — the part Mary took at this supper, where Martha served, and Lazarus sat at the table. Everything, every one, is found in the just place and season; the true light makes all manifest as it was, Jesus Himself being there, but about to die. "Mary took a pound of ointment of spikenard, very costly, and anointed the feet of Jesus." She did anoint His head, and other gospels speak of this; but John mentions what was peculiar. It was natural to anoint the head; but the special thing for the eye of love to discern was the anointing of the feet. This was specially shown in two ways.

The woman in Luke 7 did the very same thing; but this was not Mary, nor is there any good reason to suppose that it was even Mary Magdalene, any more than the sister of Lazarus. It was "a woman that was a sinner;" and I believe there is much moral beauty in not giving us her name, for obvious reasons. What could it do but become an evil precedent, besides indulging a prurient curiosity about her? The name is here dropped; but what of that, if it be written in heaven? There is a delicate veil cast over (not the grace shown by the Lord, but) the name of this woman who was a sinner; but there is an eternal record of the name and deed of Mary, the sister of Lazarus, who at this much later moment anoints the feet of Christ. Yet, as far as this goes, both women did the same thing. The one, in the abasement of feeling her sin before His ineffable love, did what Mary did in the sense of His deep glory, and with an instinctive feeling withal of some impending evil that menaced Him. Thus the sense of her sin, and the sense of His glory, brought them, as it were, to the same point. Another point of analogy is, that neither woman spoke; the heart of each expressed itself in deeds intelligible, at least, to Him who was the object of this homage, and He understood and vindicated both.

In this case the house was filled with the odour of the ointment; but this manifestation of her love who thus anointed Jesus brought out the ill-feeling and covetousness of one soul who cared not for Jesus, but was, indeed, a thief under his high pretensions of care for the poor. It is a very solemn scene in this point of view, the line of treachery alongside of the offering of grace. How often the self-same circumstances, which draw out fidelity and devotedness, manifest either heartless treachery or self-seeking and worldliness 1

Such, in brief, was the interior of Bethany. Outside Jewish rancour was undisguised. The heart of the chief priests was set on blood. The Lord, in the next scene, enters Jerusalem as the Son of David. But I must pass on, merely noting this Messianic witness in its place. When Jesus was glorified, the disciples remembered these things. The subsequent notice we have is the remarkable desire expressed by the Greeks, through Philip, to see Jesus. Here the Lord at once passes to another testimony, the Son of man, where the introduction of His most efficacious death is couched under the well-known figure of the corn of wheat falling into the ground and dying, as the harbinger, and, indeed, the means, of much fruit. In the path of His death they must follow who would be with Him. Not that here again the destined Head of all, the Son of man, is insensible at the prospect of such a death, but cries to the Father, who answers the call to glorify His name by the declaration that He had (i.e., at the grave of Lazarus), and would again (i.e., by raising up Jesus Himself).

The Lord, in the centre of the chapter just after this, opens out once more the truth of the world's judgment, and of His cross as the attractive point for all men, as such, in contrast with Jewish expectation. There is, first, perfect submission to the Father's will, whatever it may cost; then, the perception of the results in all their extent. This is followed by their unbelief in His proper glory, as much as in His sufferings. Such must ever be for man, for the world, the insuperable difficulty. They had heard it in vain in the law; for this is always misused by man, as we have seen in the gospel of John. They could not reconcile it with the voice of grace and truth. Both had been fully manifested in Jesus, and above all, would be yet more in His death. The voice of the law spoke to their ears of a Christ continuing for ever; but a Son of man humbled, dying, lifted up! Who was this Son of man? How exactly the counterpart of an Israelite's objections to this day! The voice of grace and truth was that of Christ come to die in shame, yet a sacrifice for sinners, however true also it was that in His own person He should continue for ever. Who could put these things together, seemingly so opposed? He who only heeds the law will never understand either the law or Christ.

Hence the chapter concludes with two closing warnings. Had they heard their own prophets? Let them listen also to Jesus. We have seen their ignorance of the law. In truth, the prophet Isaiah had shown long before that this was no new thing. He had predicted it in John 6, though a remnant should hear. The light of Jehovah might be ever so bright, but the heart of the people was gross. "Seeing they saw, but they did not understand." There was no reception of the light of God. Even if they believed after a sort, there was no confession to salvation, for they loved the praise of men, Jesus — the Son of God, Jehovah Himself — stands on earth and cries — His final testimony. He pronounces upon it — claims once more to be the light. He was "come a light into the world." This we have seen all through, from John 1 down to John 12. He was come a light into the world, that those that believed on Him should not abide in darkness. The effect was plain from the first; they preferred darkness to light. They loved sin; they had God manifested in love, manifested in Christ. The darkness was thus rendered only more visible in consequence of the light. "If any man hear my words, and believe not. I judge him not: for I came not to judge the world, but to save the world. He that rejecteth me, and receiveth not my words, hath one that judgeth him: the word that I have spoken, the same shall judge him in the last day." Christ had not spoken from Himself, but as the sent One from the Father, who had charged Him what to say and what to speak. "And I know that his commandment is life everlasting: whatsoever I speak therefore, even as the Father said unto me, so I speak."

Time does not admit of more than a few words on the next two chapters (John 13, 14), which introduce a distinct section of our gospel, where (testimony having been fully rendered, not indeed with hope of man, but for the glory of God,) Christ quits association with man (though supper time was come, not "ended" — ver. 2) for a place suited to His glory, intrinsic and relational, as well as conferred; but alone with this (blessed to say), to give His own a part with Him in that heavenly glory (instead of His reigning over Israel here below).

Before concluding tonight, this I can notice but briefly, in order to bring my subject within the space allotted for it. Happily, there is the less need to dwell on the chapters at the length they might claim, since many here are familiar with them, comparatively speaking. They are especially dear to the children of God in general.

First of all, our Lord has now terminated all question of testimony to man, whether to the Jew or to the world. He now addresses Himself to His own in the world, the unwavering, abiding objects of His love, as one just about to leave this world actually for that place which suits His essential nature, as well as the glory destined Him by the Father. Accordingly, our Lord, as one about to go to heaven, new to Him as man, would prove His increasing love to them, (though fully knowing what the enemy would effect through the wickedness of one of their number, as well as through the infirmity of another,) and hence proceeds to give a visible sign then of what they would only understand later. It was the service of love that He would continue for them, when Himself out of this world and themselves in it; a service as real as any that He had ever done for them while He was in this world, and if possible, more important than any they had yet experienced. But, then, this ministration of His grace was also connected with His own new portion in heaven. That is, it was to give them a part with Him outside the world. It was not divine goodness meeting them in the world, but as He was leaving the world for heaven, whence He came, He would associate them with Himself, and give them a share with Himself where He was going. He was about to pass, though Lord of all, into the presence of God His Father in heaven, but would manifest Himself the servant of them all, even to the washing of their feet soiled in walking here below. The point, therefore, was (not here exactly suffering for sins, but) the service of love for saints, to fit them for having communion with Him, before they have their portion with Him in that heavenly scene to which He was going at once. Such is the meaning suggested by the washing of the disciples' feet. In short, it is the word of God applied by the Holy Ghost to deal with all that unfits for fellowship with Christ in heaven, while He is there. It is the Holy Ghost's answer here to what Christ is doing there, as one identified with their cause above, the Holy Ghost meanwhile carrying on a like work in the disciples here, to keep them in, or restore them to, communion with Christ there. They are to be with Him alone; but, meanwhile, He is producing and keeping up, by the Spirit's use of the word, this practical fellowship with Himself on high. While the Lord, then, intimates to them that it had a mystical meaning, not apparent on the face of it, nothing could be more obvious than the love or the humility of Christ. This, and more than this, had been abundantly shown by Him already, and in His every act. This, therefore, was not, and could not be, what was here meant, as that which Peter did not know then, but should know hereafter. Indeed, the lowly love of His Master was so apparent then, that the ardent but hasty disciple stumbled over it. There ought to be neither difficulty nor hesitation in allowing that a deeper sense lay hidden under that simple but suggestive action of Jesus — a sense which not even the chief of the twelve could then divine, but which not only he, but every one else, ought to seize now that it is made good in Christianity, or, more precisely, in Christ's dealing with the defilements of His own.

This should be borne in mind, that the washing meant is not with blood, but with water. It was for those who would be already washed from their sins in His blood, but who need none the less to be washed with water also. Indeed, it were well to look more narrowly into the words of our Lord Jesus. Besides the washing with blood, that with water is essential, and this doubly. The washing, of regeneration is not by blood, though inseparable from redemption by blood, and neither the one nor the other is ever repeated. But in addition to the washing of regeneration, there is a continual dealing of grace with the believer in this world; there is the constant need of the application of the word by the Holy Ghost discovering whatever there may be of inconsistency, and bringing him to judge himself in the detail of daily walk here below.

Note the contrast between legal requirement and our Lord's action in this case. Under the law the priests washed themselves, hands as well as feet. Here Christ washes their feet. Need I say how highly the superiority of grace rises over the typical act of the law? Then follows, in connection and in contrast with it, the treachery of Judas. See how the Lord felt it from His familiar friend! How it troubled His spirit! It was a deep sorrow, a fresh instance of what has been referred to already.

Finally, at the end of the chapter, when the departure of Judas on his errand brought all before Him, the Saviour speaks again of death, and so glorifying God. It is not directly for the pardon or deliverance of disciples; yet who does not know that nowhere else is their blessing so secured? God was glorified in the Son of man where it was hardest, and even more than if sin had never been. Hence, as fruit of His glorifying God in His death, God would glorify Him in Himself "straightway." This is precisely what is taking place now. And this, it should be observed again, is in contrast with Judaism. The hope of the Jews is the manifestation of Christ's glory here below and by-and-by. What John shows is here in the immediate glorification of Christ on high. It does not depend upon any future time and circumstance, but was immediately consequent on the cross. But Christ was alone in this; none now could follow — no disciple, any more than a Jew, as Peter, bold but weak, would prove to his cost. The ark must go first into Jordan, but we may follow then, as Peter did triumphantly afterwards.

John 14 (and here, too, I must be brief) follows up the same spirit of contrast with all that belonged to Judaism; for if the ministry of love in cleansing the saints practically was very different from a glorious reign Over the earth, so was the hope here given them of Christ just as peculiar. The Lord intimates, first of all, that He was not going to display Himself now as a Jewish Messiah, visible to the world; but as they believed in God, so they were to believe in Him. He was going to be unseen: quite a new thought to the Jewish mind as regards the Messiah, who, to them, always implied One manifested in power and glory in the world. "Ye believe in God," He says, "believe also in me." But then He connects the unseen condition He was about to assume with the character of the hope He was giving them. It was virtually saying that He was not going merely to bless them here. Nor would it be a scene for man to look on with his natural eyes in this world. He was going to bless them in an infinitely better way and place. "In my Father's house are many mansions; if it were not so, I would have told you." This is what the Son tells. Very different is the burden of the prophets. This was a new thing reserved most fitly for Him. Who but He should be the first to unveil to disciples on earth the heavenly scene of love and holiness and joy and glory He knew so well? "If it were not so, I would have told you. I go to prepare a place for you. And if I go and prepare a place for you, I will come again, and receive you unto myself; that where I am, there ye may be also." This is the turning-point and secret — "where I am." All depends on this precious privilege. The place that was due to the Son was the place that grace would give to the sow. They were to be in the same blessedness with Christ. It was not merely, therefore, Christ about to depart and be in heaven, maintaining their communion with Himself there, but — wondrous grace! — in due time they, too, were to follow and be with Him; yea, if He went before them, so absolute was the grace, that He would not devolve it on any one else, so to speak to usher them there. He would come Himself, and thus would bring them into His own place — "That where I am, there ye may be also." This, I say, in all its parts, is the contrast of every hope, even of the brightest Jewish expectations.

Besides, He would assure them of the ground of their hope. In His own person they ought to have known how this could be. "Whither I go ye know, and the way ye know." They were surprised. Then, as ever, it was the overlooking of His glorious person that gave occasion to their bewilderment. In answer to Thomas, He says, "I am the way, the truth, and the life." He was the way to the Father, and therefore they ought to have known. because no man comes to the Father but by Him. By receiving Jesus, by believing in Him, and only so, one comes to the Father, whom they had seen in Him, as Philip should have known. He was the way, and there was none other. Besides, He was the truth, the revelation of every one and everything as they are. He was also the life, in which that truth was, by the Spirit's power, known and enjoyed. In every way Christ was the only possible means of their entering into this blessedness. He was in the Father, and the Father in Him; and as the words were not spoken from Himself, so the Father abiding in Him did the works. (Verses 1-11)

Then our Lord turns, from what they should even then have known in and from His person and words and works, to another thing which could not then be known. This divides the chapter. The first part is the Son known on earth in personal dignity as declaring the Father — imperfectly, no doubt, but still known. This ought to have been the means of their. apprehending whither He was going; for He was the Son not merely of Mary but of the Father. And this they then knew, however dull in perceiving the consequences. All His manifestation in this gospel was just the witness of this glory, as they certainly ought to have seen; and the new hope was thoroughly in accordance with that glory. But now he discloses to them that which they could only do and understand when the Holy Ghost was given. "Verily, verily, I say unto you, He that believeth on me, the works that I do shall he do also; and greater works than these shall he do; because I go unto my Father. And whatsoever ye shall ask in my name, that will I do, that the Father may be glorified in the Son. If ye shall ask any thing in my name, I will do it. If ye love me, keep my commandments. And I will pray the Father, and he shall give you another Comforter, that he may abide with you for ever; even the Spirit of truth; whom the world cannot receive, because it seeth him not, neither knoweth him: but ye know him; for he dwelleth with you, and shall be in you. I will not leave you comfortless: I will come to you. Yet a little while, and the world seeth me no more; but ye see me: because I live, ye shall live also. At that day ye shall know that I am in my Father, and ye in me, and I in you." This supposes the Holy Ghost given. First, it is the Son present, and the Father known in Him, and He in the Father. Next, the Holy Ghost is promised. When He was given, these would be the blessed results. He was going away indeed; but they might better prove their love by keeping His commandments, than in human grief over His absence. Besides, Christ would ask the Father, who would give them their ever-abiding Comforter while He Himself was away. The Holy Ghost would be not a passing visitor on the earth, even as the Son who had been with them for a season. He would abide for ever. His dwelling with them is in contrast with any temporary blessing; and besides, He would be in them — the expression of an intimacy which nothing human can fully illustrate.

Observe, the Lord uses the present tense both for Himself and for the Comforter — the Holy Spirit — in this chapter, in a way that will be explained shortly. In the early part of verse 2 He says about Himself, "I go to Prepare a place for you." He does not mean that He was in the act of departure, but just about to go. He uses the present to express its certainty and nearness; He then was on the point of going. So even of coming back again, where likewise He uses the present, "I come again." He does not precisely say, as in the English version, "I will come." This passage of Scripture suffices to exemplify a common idiomatic usage in Greek, as in our own and other tongues, when a thing is to be regarded as sure, and to be constantly expected. It seems to me an analogous usage in connection with the Holy Ghost — "He dwelleth with you." I apprehend that the object is simply to lay the stress on the dwelling. The Holy Ghost, when He comes, will not come and go soon after, but abide. Hence, says the Lord, Jesus, "He abideth with you" — the same word so often used for abiding throughout the chapter; and next, as we saw, "He shall be in you:" a needful word to add; for otherwise it was not implied in His abiding with them.

These, then, are the two great truths of the chapter: their future portion with Christ in the Father's house; and, meanwhile, the permanent stay of the Holy Ghost with the disciples, and this, too, as indwelling on the footing of life in Christ risen. (Ver. 19) I will not leave you comfortless: I will come to you. Yet a little while, and the world seeth me no more; but ye see me: because I live, ye shall live also. At that day ye shall know that I am in my Father, and ye in me, and I in you." Thus, having the Holy Ghost as the power of life in Him, they would know Him nearer to them, and themselves to Him, when they should know Him in the Father, than if they had Him as Messiah with them and over them in the earth. These are the two truths which the Lord thus communicates to them.

Then we have a contrast of manifestation to the disciples, and to the world, connected with another very important point — the Holy Ghost's power shown in their obedience, and drawing down a love according to the Father's government of His children. It is not merely the Father's love for His children as such, but Father and Son loving them, because of having and keeping the commandments of Jesus. This would be met by a manifestation of Jesus to the soul, such as the world knows nothing of. But the Lord explains further, that if a man loves Him, he will keep His word, and His Father will love him, "and we will come to him, and make our abode with him." (v. 23) This is not a commandment, but His word — a simple intimation of His mind or will; and, therefore, as a more thorough test, so followed by a fuller blessing. This is a beautiful difference, and of great practical value, being bound up with the measure of our attentiveness of heart. Where obedience lies comparatively on the surface, and self-will or worldliness is not judged, a commandment is always necessary to enforce it. People therefore ask, "Must I do this? Is there any harm in that?" To such the Lord's will is solely a question of command. Now there are commandments, the expression of His authority; and they are not grievous. But, besides, where the heart loves Him deeply, His word[10] will give enough expression of His will to him that loves Christ. Even in nature a parent's look will do it. As we well know, an obedient child catches her mother's desire. before the mother has uttered a word. So, whatever might be the word of Jesus, it would be heeded, and thus the heart and life be formed

---

[10] It is difficult to say why Tyndale, Cranmer, the Geneva, and the Authorised Versions give the plural form, which has no authority whatever. Wycliffe and the Rhemish, adhering to the Vulgate, happen to be right. His word has a unity of character which is of moment. He that loves Christ keeps His word; he that does not love Him keeps not His words; if he observes some of them only, other motives may operate; but if he loved Christ, he would value His word as a whole.

in obedience. And what is not the joy and power where such willing subjection to Christ pervades the soul, and all is in the communion of the Father and the Son? How little can any of us speak of it as our habitual unbroken portion!

The concluding verses (25-31) bring before them the reason of the Lord's communication, and the confidence they may repose in the Spirit, both in His own teaching them all things, and in His recalling all things which Jesus said to them. "Peace," He adds, "I leave [fruit of His very death; nor this only, but His own character of peace, what He Himself knew] with you, my peace I give unto you: not as the world giveth, give I unto you." "Not as the world," which is capricious and partial, keeping for itself even where it affects most generosity. He alone who was God could give as Jesus gave, at all cost, and what was most precious. And see what confidence He looks for, what affections superior to self! "Ye have heard how I said unto you, I go away, and come again unto you. If ye loved me, ye would rejoice, because I said, I go unto the Father: for my Father is greater than I." Little remained for Him to talk with them. Another task was before Him — not with saints, but with Satan, who coming would find nothing in Him, save, indeed, obedience up to death itself, that the world might know that He loves the Father, and does just as He commands. And then He bids the disciples rise up, and go hence, as in John 13. He rose up Himself (both being, in my opinion, significant actions, in accordance with what was opening out before Him and them).

But I need and must say no more now on this precious portion. I could only hope to convey the general scope of the contents, as well as their distinctive character. May our God and Father grant that what has been said may help His children to read His word with ever deepening intelligence and enjoyment of it, and of Him with whose grace and glory it is filled!

JOHN 15-21

In John 15 our Lord substitutes Himself for Israel, as the plant of God, responsible to bear fruit for Him on earth (not merely for man, as such, openly sinful and lost). He takes the place of that which most put itself forward as being according to God here below. As our Lord Himself said (in John 4), "Salvation is of the Jews:" this place of privilege and promise made their actual condition so much the guiltier. Our Lord, therefore, sets aside openly, and forever, as regards those that He was now calling out of the world, all connection with Israel. "I am the true vine," He says. We all know that Israel of old is called the vine — the vine that the Lord had brought out of Egypt. But Israel was empty, fruitless, false: Christ was the only true vine. Whatever might be the responsibility of Israel, whatever their boasted privileges (and they really were much every way), whatever the associations and hopes of the chosen people, all outside Christ had fallen under the power of the adversary. The only blessing for a soul now was found in Christ Himself; and so He opens the discourse (or, as we saw, closes what went before) with — "Rise up: let us go hence." There was an abandonment, not only for Himself, but for them, of all connection with nature, or the world, even in their religion. It was Christ now, or nothing. As in the beginning of John 13, He had risen up anticipatively as a sign of His work for them on high; so here He calls them to quit all their earthly belongings with Himself; they were now definitively done with. Thus we have the Lord taking now the place substitutionally of all that had exercised religious power over their spirits. It was now proved to be neither a blessing nor even safety for a soul on earth.

"I," He says, "am the true vine, and my Father is the husbandman." He puts Himself in the place of all to which they had been attached and belonged here below, and the Father in lieu of Almighty God, or the Jehovah of Israel. So had He been known. to the fathers and the children of Israel; but it was His Father, as such, to whose care He commends them now. "Every branch in me that beareth not fruit;" for fruit was what God looked for, not merely acts or obligations, but bearing fruit: "Every branch in me that beareth not fruit he taketh away; and every branch that beareth fruit, he purgeth it, that it may bring forth more fruit." This is the general statement. There is a two-fold dealing with those who took the place of being branches of the true vine. Where no fruit was borne, there was judgment in excision; where fruit appeared, purging followed, that there might be more.

The Lord applies this truth particularly: "Already ye are clean through the word that I have spoken to you. Exhortation follows in verses 4, 5; the results distinctively for "a man," for any one (τις) who does not abide, and for the disciples who do, are found respectively in verse 6, and in verses 7, 8.

In this chapter it is never simply a question of divine grace saving sinners, blotting out iniquities, remembering sins and transgressions no more; but the power of the word is morally applied to judge whatever is contrary to God's character displayed in Christ, or, rather, to the Father's will revealed in Him. No standard less than this could be entertained, now that Christ was revealed. They then (for Judas was gone) were already clean through the word Christ had spoken to them. The law of Moses, divine as it was, would not suffice: it was negative; but Christ's word is positive. "Abide in me, and I in you. As the branch cannot bear fruit of itself, except it abide in the vine; no more can ye, except ye abide in me." It is not what God is in grace towards those that are outside Him and lost, but the appraisal of the ways of those associated with Christ, the dealings of God, or more strictly of His Father, with those who professed to belong to the Lord. I say "professed," because it is to me evident that He does not contemplate in His view those exclusively who really had life everlasting. Still less do branches of the vine mean the same thing as members of Christ's body, but His followers, who might even abandon Him, as some in the earliest days walked no more with Him. This alone explains our chapter, without forcing it.

The Lord, then, has in view those who then surrounded Him, already branches in the vine, and, of course, in principle, all that should follow, including those that would nominally, and at first to all appearance really, abandon Israel and all things for Him. It was no light matter, but one of much seriousness; and surely, therefore, if a man did thus come out from all that claimed his affections and conscience, from his religion; in short, if a man came out at the cost of every thing, finding most of all foes in those of his own household, there was that which presumed sincerity of conduct, but had still to be proved. The proof would be abiding in Christ. There is no word more characteristic of John than the very word "abiding," and this in the way both of grace and of government. Here it is the disciples put to the proof. For Christianity is the revelation, not of a dogma, but of a person who has wrought redemption; doubtless, also, of a person in whom is life, and who gives it. Thence flows a new sort of responsibility; and a very important thing it is to see this most strikingly kept up in him, who, of all the evangelists, most strongly brings in the absolute unconditional love of God. Take the early part of the gospel, where the gift of Jesus in divine love, the sending Him into the world not to judge, but to save, makes known what God is to a lost world. There we have grace without a single thought of any thing on man's part, save the depth of need. "For God," He says, "so loved the world, that he gave his only begotten Son, that whosoever believeth in him should not perish, but have everlasting life. For God sent not his Son into the world to condemn the world; but that the world through him might be saved." (John 3:16, 17) But here the ground is different. We see those who had come out to Christ from all that they had previously valued in the earth. Alas! flesh is capable of imitating faith; it can go a long way in religiousness, and in renunciation of the profane world. Soon there would be multitudes who would come out from Israel and be baptized unto Christ; but still they must be fully tested. None would stand by baptism, or by any other ordinance, but by abiding in Christ.

"Abide in me, and I in you." Here He always puts man's part first, because it is a question, as we have seen, of responsibility; where it is the grace of God, His part is first necessarily, and, further, it necessarily abides. Whereas, if man's responsibility is before us, it is evident that there can be no necessary permanence here: all turns on dependence on Him who always abides the same yesterday, today, and for ever. Thus the reality of God's work in the soul proves itself, so to speak, by continual looking and clinging to Christ. In verse 4 it is not, "Except I abide in you," but, "Except ye abide in me."

"I am the vine, and ye are the branches: he that abideth in me, and I in him, the same bringeth forth much fruit: for without me ye can do nothing." (Verse 5) It is not here believing, but "doing," though faith be the spring, of course. The Lord would have us bear much fruit, and the only way in which fruit is to be borne is by abiding in Him in whom we believe. What can be a weightier consideration for us, after receiving Christ! Do you go after some other thing or person in order to bear fruit? The result in God's sight is bad fruit.

Thus Christ is not only everlasting life to the soul that believes in Him, but He is the only source of fruit-bearing, all the course through, for those that have received Him. The secret is the heart occupied with Him, the soul dependent on Him, Himself the object in all trials, difficulties, and duties even; so that, though a given thing be a duty, it be not done now barely as such, but with Christ before the eye of faith. But where there is not a life exercised in self-judgment and in enjoyment of Christ. as well as prayer, men get tired of this; they turn away from Him to the nostrums of the day, whether novel or antique, moral or intellectual. They find their attraction in religious feelings, experiences, frames, or visions; in imagining some new good self, or in anatomizing the old bad self; in sacerdotalism, ordinances, or legalism, of one sort or another. Thus they really return, in some shape or degree, to the false vine, instead of cleaving to the true. They lose themselves thus. It may even be a slip back into the world, into the open enemy of the Father; for this is no uncommon result, where there is for a time an abandonment of the old fleshly vine, the religion of ordinances, of human effort, and of assumed privilege. All this was found in its fulness and apparent perfection in Israel; but it was now discovering its utter hopeless hollowness and antagonism to the mind of God; and this was manifested, as we shall find later on in this chapter, in their causeless hatred of the Father and the Son. Christ is ever the test, and this the close declares, as much as the beginning sets Him forth as the only power of preparing for, and producing fruit.

This appears again in the sixth verse, and remarkably too: "If a man abide not in me, he is cast forth as a branch." Apply such language to life everlasting, or, still more, to union with Christ, and there is nothing but endless confusion. Where Scripture speaks of union with Christ, or, again, of life in Him, you never have such a thought as a member of Christ cut off, or one that had eternal life losing it. It is very possible that some who have accurate knowledge might give it, or plunge into all; and this is what Peter speaks of in his second epistle. There is no preservative energy in knowledge ever so full. Such might allow stumbling-blocks, disappointments, etc., to hinder their following Christ, and so practically abandon what they know, the result of which would be the surest and most disastrous ruin. They are worse even than before. So Jude speaks of men twice dead; and, in fact, experience proves that men who have no life in Christ, after having professed awhile, become fiercer adversaries, if not grosser sinners, against the Lord than before any such profession was made.

This is the case our Lord describes here: "If a man abide not in me, he is cast forth as a branch, and is withered; and they gather them, and cast them into the fire, and they are burned." It was one who had come out from the world, and had followed Christ. But there was no attraction of heart, no power of faith, and consequently no dependence on Christ; and this is the Lord's sentence pronounced on all such, whether in that day or in any other.

On the other hand, He says, "If ye abide in me, and my words abide in you, ye shall ask what ye will, and it shall be done unto you." Not only is the heart occupied with Christ, but also His words weigh there. The Old Testament alone would not suffice. It had been used of God when there was nothing more. Blessed of God at all times it would surely be; and he that valued Christ's words would never slight those that witnessed of Christ before He came. But the soul that would make light of the words of Christ, or do without them, after they were communicated, would evince its own faithlessness. The Christian that really prizes the word of God in the Old Testament would still more set his heart on that in the New. He that had no more than a naturally reverent attachment to the law and the prophets, without faith, would prove his real condition by inattention to Christ's words. Thus, to this day, the Jews are themselves the great witness of the truth of our Lord's warning. They are clinging to the empty vine; and so all their religious profession is as empty before God. They may seem to cleave to the words of Moses, but it is mere human tenacity, not divine faith: else the words of Christ would be welcome above all. As the Lord had told them at an earlier moment, had they believed Moses, they would have believed Christ. for Moses wrote of Christ: in truth, there was no divine persuasion as to either. Again, the great test now is Christ's words abiding in us. Old truth, even though equally of God as the new, ceases to be a test when new truth is given and refused, or slighted; and the same thing is true not merely of God's word as a whole, but of a particular truth, when God reawakens it at any given time for the actual exigency of the Church or of His work. It is vain, for instance, to fall back now on the principles put forward and acted on two or three hundred years ago. Of course it is right and of God to hold fast all He gave at any time; but if there be real faith, it will be found out ere long that the Holy Ghost has before Him the present need for the Lord's glory in the Church; and those that have real confidence in His power will not merely hold fast the old but accept the new, in order so much the more to walk in communion with Him who ever watches and works for the name of Christ and the blessing of His saints.

In this case, however, it is the larger subject — the all-importance of Christ's words abiding in us: "If ye abide in me, and my words abide in you." There is first the person, then the expression of His mind. Prayer follows: "Ye shall ask what ye will, and it shall be done unto you." It is not prayer first (for this should not take the place either of Christ or of intelligence in His mind), but Christ Himself, the prime object; then His words, as forming fully the heart, according to His thoughts and will; and, lastly, the going out of the heart to the Father, on the ground both of Christ and of His revealed mind, with the annexed assurance that so it should come to pass for them. (Verse 7)

The prayer of Christians is often far from this. How many prayers are there where nothing seems to be done! This way be true, not merely of poor failing souls, such as any of us here; but even an apostle might find the same thing in his course, and God Himself be the witness of it. Indeed, the apostle Paul is the chronicler of the fact to us, that his prayers were not always in this communion. We know he besought the Lord thrice to take away that which was an immense trial to him, making him despicable in the eyes of the less spiritual. We can understand this: nothing is more natural; but, for that very reason, it was not all in the power of the Spirit of God, with Christ as the first object. He was thinking of himself, of his brethren, and of the work; but God graciously brought him to Christ, as the One sustained and sustaining object — to abide in Him, as it is said here, and to have Christ's words abiding in himself, and then all the resources of God were at his command. "And he said unto me, My grace is sufficient for thee; for my strength is made perfect in weakness. Most gladly, therefore, will I rather glory in my infirmities, that the power of Christ may rest upon me." (Compare also Phil. 4:6-13) It is only so that there is the certainty of the answer, at least, of what we ask being done.

The object is to show how God the Father answers and acts in accordance with those who are thus practically associated in heart with Christ. And so it is written, "Herein is my Father glorified, that ye bear much fruit, and ye shall become my disciples." (Verse 8) "Disciples," be it noted; for we must carefully bear in mind that we have not the Church as such here, and, indeed, we have never the Church, strictly speaking, in John. The reason is manifest, because the object of this gospel is not to point out Christ in heaven, but God manifesting Himself in Christ on the earth. I do not mean that we have no allusion to His ascent or presence there; for we have seen that there is here some such allusion, especially when the Holy Ghost replaces Him here, and we shall have it repeatedly in what follows. At the same time, the main testimony of John is not so much Christ as man in heaven, but God in Him manifest on the earth. It is evident that, He being the Son, the special place of privilege found in the gospel of John is that of children — not members of Christ's body, but sons of God, as receiving and associated with the Son, the only-begotten Son of the Father.

Here He speaks of them as disciples; for, in point of fact, the relationship of which John 15 speaks was already true. They had already come to Christ; they had forsaken all to follow Him, and were then around Him. He was the Vine now and here. It was not a new place He was going to enter. They, too, were branches then, and more than that, they were clean through the word He had spoken to them. Not that they were then cleansed by blood, but, at least, they were born of water and of the Spirit. They had this cleansing, this moral operation, of the Spirit wrought in their souls. They were bathed or washed all over, and henceforth needed not save to wash their feet.

"As the Father hath loved me, so have I loved you: continue [abide] ye in my love." (Ver. 9) It is all a question of the Father's government and the disciples' responsibility; not of a people having to do with a governor nationally, as Jehovah was to Israel, but of Christ's disciples in relation with the Father, according to the revelation of Himself in Christ. Nor is it here His grace delivering souls, but, what is true along with that, the full maintenance of individual responsibility, according to the manifestation of His nature and relationship in Christ here below. Thus, as compared with the past, the standard is raised immensely. For when once God had brought out Christ, He neither could nor would go back to anything less. It is not merely that He could not own anything short of Christ as a means of salvation, because this is always true; and never was any one brought to God at any time since the world began save by Christ, however scanty the testimony or partial the knowledge of Him. Under the law there was, comparatively speaking, little or no acquaintance with His work as a distinct thing, nor could there be, perhaps (at any rate there was not), even after He came, till the work was done. But here we have God's ways and character as manifested in Christ, and nothing less than this would suit His disciples, or be agreeable to the Father. As already remarked, the application of this to life everlasting only induces contradiction. Thus, if we suppose that the subject of the chapter is, e.g., life or union with Christ, just see into what difficulties this false start plunges one at once: all would be made conditional, and those united to Christ might be lost. "If ye keep my commandments" — what has that to do with life eternal in Christ? Does union with Christ, does life eternal, depend on keeping His commandments? Clearly not; yet there is a meaning, and a most weighty meaning for those that belong to Christ, in these words. Apply them, not to grace but to government, and all is plain and sure and consistent.

The meaning is, that it is impossible to produce fruit for the Father, — impossible to keep up the enjoyment of Christ's love, unless there be obedience, and this to Christ's commandments. I repeat, that he who values the Master will not despise the servant; but there are many who do acknowledge their responsibility to the law of Moses without appreciating and obeying the words of Christ. He that loves Christ will enjoy all truth, because Christ is the truth. He will cherish every expression of God's mind; he will find guidance in the law, the prophets, the psalms — everywhere; and so much the more where there is the fullest revelation of Christ Himself. Christ is the true light. Therefore, as long as Christ is not the One in and through whose light the Scriptures, whether old or new, are read, a man is but groping his way in the dark. When he sees and believes in the Son, there is for him a sure way through the wilderness, and also a bright way in the word of God. The darkness passes away; bondage is no more; there is no condemnation, but, on the contrary, life, light, and liberty; but, at the same time, it is a liberty used in the sense of responsibility to please our God and Father, measured by the revelation of Himself in Christ.

So the Lord says, "If ye keep my commandments, ye shall abide in my love; even as I have kept my Father's commandments, and abide in his love." The consequence is, that where there is carelessness in one who belongs to Christ, in a living, branch of the vine, the Father as the husbandman deals in purging judgment. Where habitual obedience is found, there is habitual enjoyment of Christ's love. "These things have I spoken unto you, that my joy might remain in you, and that your joy might be full."

Supposing that for a time there is a departure from Christ, what is the effect of it? No matter how really a man may be a child of God, he is miserable; the more real, the more miserable. One that had not a conscience exercised before God might sleep over sin and accustom himself to evil for a while; and an unreal disciple would grow. tired of carrying on the profession of Christ along with indulged evil; nor would God allow it to go beyond a certain point as an ordinary rule. But for a saint, true-hearted in the main, nothing is more certain than that Christ would deal with him, and that he would lose meanwhile all sense of the love of Christ as a present practical thing. It is a matter of communion, not of salvation. And surely it ought to be so, and we would not desire it to be otherwise. Who would desire an unreal thing — the keeping up an appearance, the parade of words and sentiments beyond the heart's state? There is nothing more calamitous for a soul than to be going on badly, and withal keeping up a vain, exaggerated semblance of feeling, where there is a scanty answer to it within.

With the enjoyment of Christ's love, then, goes obedience; and where the disciple fails in obedience, there cannot be a real abiding in His love. Here it is not a question of love everlasting, but of present communion. He only abides in Christ's love who walks in His will faithfully. We must discriminate in the love of Christ. Unconditionally, of pure grace, He loved them that were His. Again, there was love, in a broad sense even for those that were not His, as we have seen more than once. Besides, there is the special personal love of approbation for him who is walking in the ways of God.

Some there are a little sensitive on these subjects. They do not like to hear, save of eternal love of the elect; and certainly, if this were weakened or denied, they might have reason to resent it. But as it is there cannot be a more painful proof of their own state. The reason why they cannot bear this farther truth is because it condemns them. If these things are in Scripture, (and deny them who dares?) our business is to submit; our duty is to seek to understand them; our wisdom is to correct and challenge ourselves, if peradventure we find insubjection within us to anything that concerns Him and our own souls. Not to speak of Christ, even on the lowest ground, we are depriving ourselves of what is good and profitable. What, indeed, can be more ruinous than putting aside that which condemns any state in which we find ourselves?

I need not enter into all the details of our chapter, though I have rather minutely gone over it thus far, believing it to be of special importance, because it is so much and generally misunderstood. Here the Lord presents Himself as the only source, not of life, as elsewhere, but of fruit-bearing for disciples, or His professed followers. What He shows is, that they need Him just as much for every day as for eternity; that they need Him for the fruit the Father expects from them now, just as much as for a title to heaven. Hence He speaks of that which pertains to a disciple on the earth; and accordingly the Lord speaks of having Himself kept His Father's commandments, and of His own abiding in His love; for, indeed, He had ever been here below the dependent man, to whom the Father was the moral source of the life He lived; and so He would have us now to live because of Himself.

I entreat any who have misread this chapter to examine thoroughly what I am now urging on my hearers. It is incalculable the quantity of scripture that is passed over without distinct exercise of faith. Souls receive it in a general way; and too often one reason why it is received so easily is, because they do not face the truth, and their conscience is not exercised by it. If they thought, weighed, and let into their souls the real truth conveyed, they might at first be startled, but the way and the end would be blessed to them. What a return for these wondrous communications of Christ, just to slip over them perfunctorily, without making the light our own! Our Lord then clearly shows that He, as man here below, had Himself walked under the government of His Father. It was not merely that He was born of a woman, born under the law, but, as He says here, "Even as I have kept my Father's commandments." It went much farther than the ten words, or all the rest of the law; it embraced every expression of the Father's authority, from whatever quarter it came. And as He could not but perfectly keep His Father's commandments, He abode in His love. As the eternal Son of the Father, of course He was ever loved of the Father; as laying down His life (John 10), He was therefore loved of His Father; but, besides, in all His earthly path, He kept His Father's commandments, and abode in His love. The Father, looking upon the Son as man walking here below, never found the slightest deflection; but, on the contrary, the perfect image of His own will in Him who, being the Son, made known and glorified the Father as He never was nor could be by any other. This was not simply as God, but rather as the Man Christ Jesus here below. I admit that, being such an One, there could be no failure. To suppose I will not say the fact, but the possibility even, of a flaw in Christ, either as God or as man, proves that he who admits the thought has no faith in His person. There could be none. Still, the trial was made under the most adverse circumstances; and He who, though God Himself, was at the same time man, walked as man perfectly, as truly as He was perfect man; and thus the Father's love rested governmentally upon Him fully, unwaveringly, absolutely in all His ways.

Now we, too, are placed upon the true ground as the disciples, strictly speaking, who were then there; but, of course, the same principle applies to all.

Another thing comes in after this. Gathered round Christ, the disciples were called on by Christ to love one another. (Ver. 12) Loving one's neighbour was not the point now; nor is it so here. Of course, loving one's neighbour abides always, but this, no matter how accomplished, ought not to be enough for a disciple of Christ. Such a demand was right and seasonable for a man in the flesh — for a Jew especially; but it could not suffice for the heart of a Christian, and, in fact, he who denies this, quarrels with the Lord's own words. A Christian, I repeat, is not absolved from loving his neighbour — nobody means that, I trust; but what I affirm is, that a Christian is called to love his fellow Christian in a new and special manner, exemplified and formed by the love of Christ; and I cannot but think that he who confounds this with love to his neighbour has a great deal to learn about Christ, and Christianity too.

The Lord evidently introduces it as a new thing. "This is my commandment." It was His commandment specially. He it was that first gathered the disciples. They were a distinct company from Israel, though not yet baptized into one body; but they were gathered by Christ, and round Himself, severed from the rest of the Jews so far. "This is my commandment, that ye love one another." But according to what measure? "As I have loved you. Greater love hath no man than this, that a man lay down his life for his friends." Shall I be told that any man ever loved, before Christ came into the world, as He loved? If a man will be ignorant, let him be ignorant, and show his unbelief by such an assertion, if he will. Now I say that there is a love looked for, such as could only be since Christ manifested it, and that His love fills and fashions after its own nature and direction. The disciples were now to love one another according to the pattern of Him who laid down His life for them as His friends. Indeed, He died for them when they were enemies; but this is out of sight here. They were His friends, if they did whatever He commanded them. (Ver. 14) He called them friends, not slaves; for the slave knows not what his master does; but He called them friends, for He made them His confidants in all He had heard of His Father. They had not chosen Him, but He them, and set them to go and bear fruit, abiding fruit, that He might give them whatsoever they asked the Father in His name. 'These things I command you, that ye love one another." (Verses 15-17)

And truly they would need the love of one another, as Christ loved them. They had become objects of the hatred of the world. (Verses 18, 19) The Jews knew no such experience. They might be disliked of the Gentiles. They were a peculiar people, no doubt, and the nations could ill brook a small nation raised to such a conspicuous place, whose law condemned them and their gods. But the disciples were to have the hatred of the world, of the Jew as much or more than of the Gentile. They had this indeed already, and they must make up their minds to it from the world. The love of Christ was on them, and, working in them and by them, would make them the objects of the world's hatred, and after that sort which He had Himself known. As He says here: "If the world hate you, ye know that it hated me before it hated you. If ye were of the world, the world would love his own: but because ye are not of the world, but I have chosen you out of the world, therefore the world hateth you." I refer to this for the purpose of showing, that the revelation of Christ has brought in not merely a total change in the consciousness of eternal life and salvation when the work was done, as well as the overthrow of all distinctions between Jew and Gentile, which we find, of course, in the epistles — but, besides that practically, has 'brought in a power of producing fruit that could not be before, a mutual love peculiar to Christians, and a rejection and hatred from the world beyond all that had been. In every way possible Christ gives us now His own portion, from the world as well as from the Father. "Remember the word that I said unto you, The servant is not greater than his lord. If they have persecuted me, they will also persecute you; if they have kept my saying, they will keep yours also." (Verse 20)

Fully do I admit that there were works of faith, deeds of righteousness, holy, wise, obedient ways, in saints of God from the beginning. You could not have faith without a new nature, nor this again without the exercise practically of that which was according to God's will. Therefore, as all saints from the beginning had faith, and were regenerate, so also there were spiritual ways in accordance with it.

But God's revelation in Christ makes an immense accession of blessing; and the consequence is, that this brings out the mind of God in a way that was not and could not have been before, just because there was no manifestation of Christ, and nobody but Christ could bring it adequately out. With this revelation the hatred of the world is commensurate; and the Lord puts it in the strongest possible way. "But all these things will they do unto you for my name's sake, because they know not him that sent me. If I had not come and spoken unto them, they had not had sin." (Ver. 21, 22) What can be plainer than the enormous change that was coming in now? We know that there had been sin all along, in the dealings of God with His ancient people; but what does the Lord here mean? Are we to fritter away the meaning of His language? Are we not to believe that, whatever there was before, the revelation of Christ brought sin to such a head, that what had been before was, comparatively speaking, a little thing when put beside the evil that was done against, and measured by, the glory of Christ the Son, the rejection of the Father's love; in short, the hatred shown to grace and truth — yea, the Father and the Son fully revealed in the Lord Jesus? Clearly so. It is not, then, a question of judging sin by right and wrong, by law, or by conscience — all well and in place for Israel and man as such. But when One who is more than man comes into the world, the dignity of the person sinned against, the love and light revealed in His person, all bear on the estimate of sin; and the consequence is, there could be no such character of sin till Christ was manifested, though, of course, heart and nature are the same.

But the revelation of Christ forced everything to a point, sounded the condition of man as nothing else could, and proved that, bad as Israel might be, when measured by a law — a holy, just, good law of God, yet, measured now by the Son of God, all sin previously was as nothing compared with the still deeper sin of rejecting the Son of God. "He that hateth me hateth my Father also." (Ver. 23) It is not merely God as such, but "my Father" that was hated. "If I had not done among them" — not now His words only, but works — "if I had not done among them the works which none other man did, they had not had sin: but now have they both seen and hated both me and my Father." (Verse 24) There was a full testimony, as we have seen already, in John 8, 9. (His words in John 8, His works in John 9); but the manifestation of His words and of His works only brought out man thoroughly hating the Father and the Son. Had they only failed to meet the requirements of God, as man had done under the law, there was ample provision to meet him in mercy and power; but now, under this revelation of grace, man, and Israel most of all, the world (for in this they are all merged now) stood out in open hostility to, and implacable hatred of, the fullest display of divine goodness here below. But this dreadful hopeless hatred, evil as it was, ought not to surprise one who believes the word of God; it was, "that the word might be fulfilled which was written in their law, They hated me without a cause." (Verse 25) There is nothing that so demonstrates man's total alienation and enmity. This is precisely what Christ here urges. The disciples accordingly, having received this grace in Christ, were called into a like path with Him, the epistle here below of Christ who is above. Fruit-bearing is the great point throughout John 15, as the end of it and John 16 bring before us testimony. "When the Comforter is come, whom I will send unto you from the Father, even the Spirit of truth, which proceedeth from the Father, he shall testify of me: and ye also shall bear witness, because ye have been with me from the beginning." Here is a twofold testimony — that of the disciples who had seen Christ and heard His words. Hence they were called to bear witness of Him — "because ye have been with me from the beginning." It was not only the great manifestation at the end, but the truth from the beginning, grace and truth always in Him. Dealing differently, no doubt, according to that which was before Him; still it was in Christ ever the value of what came, not what He found, which was the great point. And to this testimony (for He is showing now the full testimony which the disciples were called to render) the Holy Ghost would add His, (wondrous to say and know it true!) as distinct from the witness of the disciples. We know right well that a disciple only renders testimony by the power of the Holy Ghost. How, then, do we find the Holy Ghost's testimony spoken of as distinct from theirs? Both are true, especially when we bear in mind that He would testify of the heavenly side of truth. In John 14:26, it was said, "The Comforter, which is the Holy Ghost, whom the Father will send in my name, he shall teach you all things, and bring all things to your remembrance, whatsoever I have said unto you." There the Holy Ghost is both a teacher and helper. As it is said, "He will teach you all things" — what they never knew, besides bringing to remembrance things that they had known.

In the end of John 15 there is a good deal more. The Holy Ghost, "when he is come," (not "whom the Father will send," but) "whom I will send from the Father." (Ver. 26) The Holy Ghost was both sent by the Father, and sent by the Son; not the same thing, but quite consistent. There is a distinct line of truth in the two cases. You could not transplant from John 15 into John 14, nor the reverse, without dislocating the whole order of the truth. Surely it all deserves to be weighed, and demands from us that we should wait upon God to learn His precious things. In John 14 it is evidently the Father giving another Comforter to the disciples, and sending Him in Christ's name: Christ is looked at there as One who prays, and whose value acts for the disciples. But in John 15 it is One who is Himself everything for the disciples from on high. Here He was the one spring of whatever fruit was borne, and He is gone on high, but is the same there; and so not merely asks the Father to send, but Himself sends them from the Father the Spirit of truth, who proceeds from with the Father, if so literal a turn may be allowed. His own personal glory on high is in full view, and so He speaks and acts, while the connection with the Father is always kept up. Still, in the one case it is the Father who sends; in the other, the Son; and this last, where the point is to show the new glory of Christ above. "He shall testify of me, and ye also shall bear witness, because ye have been with me from the beginning." There would be the testimony of the Holy Ghost sent from the Son, and bearing witness of Him according to the place whence He came to replace Him here. The Holy Ghost, sent thus from above, would bear witness of the Son in heaven; but the disciples also would bear witness of what they knew when He was upon the earth, because they had been with Him from the beginning (i.e. of His manifestation here). Both we have in Christianity, which not only maintains the testimony of Christ, as manifested on the earth, but also the Holy Ghost's witness of Christ known on high. To leave out either is to strip Christianity of half its value. There is that which never can make up for Christ on the earth; and certainly there is that revealed of Christ in heaven which no manifestation on the earth can supply. They have, both of them, a divine place and power for the children of God.

John 16 seems to be based rather on this last. The main difference is, that the Holy Ghost is more spoken of here apart from the question of who sends. It is more the Holy Ghost coming than sent here; that is, the Holy Ghost is looked at — not certainly as acting independently, but yet as a distinct person. He comes, not to display His own power and glory, but expressly to glorify Christ. At the same time, He is looked at in more distinct personality than in John 14, 15. And our Lord had the wisest reason for making known to the disciples what they had to expect. They were now entering on the path of testimony, that always involves suffering We have seen what should befall them in bearing fruit as Christ's disciples and friends. This is enough for the world, which hates them as Him, because they are not of it, but are loved and chosen of Christ. These two things unite the disciples. The hatred of the world and the love of Christ press them so much the more together. But there is also the hatred which befalls them in testifying, not as disciples so much as witnesses. Witnessing as the disciples did of what they had known of Christ here, witnessing of what the Spirit taught them of Christ on high, the consequence would be, "They shall put you out of the synagogues: yea, the time cometh, that whosoever killeth you will think that he doeth God service." It is clearly religious rancour created by this full testimony, not the world's general ill-feeling, but special hatred to their testimony. Hence, it would be putting them, not merely into prisons, but out of the synagogues; and this under the notion of doing God service. It is religious persecution. "And these things will they do unto you, because they have not known the Father, nor me. How perfectly the truth shines here on Christian as well as on Jewish hatred of all full testimony to Christ! Spite of the liberalism of the day, this peeps out where it dares. They talk about God; they speculate about the Deity, providence, fate, or chance. They may even be zealous for the law, and tack on Christ to it. There a great deal of the world's religion ends. But they know not the Father nor the Son. It is irreverence to draw near and cry, Abba, Father! It is presumption for a man in this life to count himself a child of God! The consequence is, that wherever there is this ignorance of the Father and the Son, there is inveterate hostility against such as are joyful in the communion of the Father and the Son. This hatred every true witness, without compromise, and separate from the world, must more or less experience. The Lord would not have them surprised. Jewish brethren might have thought that, having received Christ, everything was to be smooth, bright, and peaceful. Not so. They must expect special and increasing, and, worst of all, religious hatred. (Verses 1-4)

"But now I go my way to him that sent me." The path lay through death, no doubt; but He puts it as going to Him that sent Him. Let them be comforted, then, as surely they would if they rightly thought of His Father's presence. But "none of you asketh me, Whither goest thou?" (Ver. 5) They felt natural sadness at the thought of His departure. Had they gone a step farther, and asked whither He was going, it would have been all right, they would have felt glad for Him; for though it were their loss, it was most surely His gain and joy — the joy that was set before Him, the joy of being with His Father, with the comfort for His own of an accomplished redemption (attested by His thus going on high). "But because I have said these things unto you, sorrow hath filled your heart. Nevertheless I tell you the truth; It is expedient for you that I go away: for if I go not away, the Comforter will not come unto you." (Ver. 7) It is the Comforter coming. No doubt Christ sends; and there lies the connection with the end of John 15. Still there is the special form of presenting Him as one that comes, which is confirmed in the next verse. "And when he is come, he will reprove [or convince] the world of sin, and of righteousness, and of judgment." (Ver. 8) This is a sentence much to be pondered. It is now God's Spirit dealing according to the gospel with individual souls, which is perfectly true and most important. Conviction of sin is wrought in all who are born of God. What confidence could there be in a soul professing to have found redemption, even forgiveness of sins, through His blood, unless there were an accompanying sense of sin? The Spirit of God does produce this. Souls must be simple and distinct in it as truly as in believing in Christ Jesus. There is a real individual work in those, yea, in all brought to God. For a sinner, repentance remains an eternal necessity.

Here, however, the Holy Ghost is not spoken of as dealing with individuals when He regenerates them and they believe, but as bringing conviction to the world of sin because of unbelief There is no real conviction of sin unless there be faith. It may be but the first working of God's grace in the soul that produces it. There may not be faith so as to have peace with God, but assuredly enough to judge of one's own ways and condition before God; and this is precisely the way in which He does ordinarily work. At the same time there is also the conviction of which the Lord speaks: The Holy Ghost, when He is come, will convince the world of sin. Why? Because they have broken the law? Not so. This may be used, but is not the ground nor the standard when Christ is the question. The law remains, and the Spirit of God often employs it, specially if a man be in self-righteousness. But the fact is clear, that the Holy Ghost is sent down; as it is also clear, that the Holy Ghost, being here, convicts the world — i.e., what is outside where He is. Were there faith, the Holy Ghost would be in their midst; but the world does not believe. Hence Christ is, as everywhere in John, the standard for judging the condition of men. "When he is come, he will convince the world of sin, and of righteousness, and of judgment: of sin, [not when they begin to believe in me, but] because they believe not in me." Again, the conviction of righteousness is equally remarkable. There is no reference even to the blessed Lord when on earth, or to what He did here. "Of righteousness, because I go to my Father, and ye see me no more." (Verses 8-10)

Thus there is a twofold conviction of righteousness. The first ground is, that the only righteousness now is in Christ gone to be with the Father. So perfectly did Christ glorify God in death, as He always did in life the things that pleased His Father, that nothing short of putting Him as man at His own right hand could meet the case. Wondrous fact! a man now in glory, at the right hand of God, above all angels, principalities, and powers. This is the proof of righteousness. It is what God the Father owed to Christ, who had so perfectly pleased and so morally glorified Him, even in respect of sin. All the world, yea, all worlds, would be too little to mark His sense of value for Christ and His work — nothing less than setting Him as man at His right hand in heaven. But there is another though negative, as that was the positive, proof of righteousness — that the world has lost Christ, "and ye see me no more." When Christ returns, He will gather His own to Himself, as in John 14. But as for the world, it has rejected and crucified Christ. The consequence is, that it will see Christ no more till He comes in judgment, and this will be to put down its pride for ever. Thus there is this double conviction of righteousness: the first is Christ gone to be with the Father on high; the second is Christ seen no more consequently. The rejected Christ is accepted and glorified in the highest seat above, which condemns the world and proves there is no righteousness in it or man; but more than this, the world shall see Him no more. When He returns, it is to judge man; but as far as concerns the offer of blessing to man in a living Christ, it is gone for ever. The Jews did and do look for Him; but when He came, they would not have Him. The best of the world, therefore, the choicest and most divinely privileged of men, have turned out the most guilty. A living Messiah they will never see. If any have Him now, it can only be a rejected and heavenly Christ.

But there is another thing — the Spirit will convince the world "of judgment." What is the conviction of judgment? It is not the destruction of this place or that. Such was the way in which God manifested His judgment of old; but the Holy Ghost bears witness now, that the prince of this world is judged. He led the world to cast out the truth, and God Himself, in the person of Christ. His judgment is sealed. It is fixed beyond hope of change.

It is only a question of the moment in God's hands, and the world with its prince will be treated according to the judgment already pronounced. "Of judgment," He says, "because the prince of this world is judged." (Verse 11) In John we have the truth, without waiting for what will be manifest. The Spirit here judges things at the roots, dealing with things according to their reality in God's sight, into which the believer enters.

Thus everywhere there is absolute opposition between the world and the Father, expressed morally when the Son was here, and proved now that the Spirit is come. The great mark of the world is that the Father is unknown. Hence, like Jews, or even heathen, they can pray to Almighty God to bless their leagues, or their arms, their crops, their herds, or what not. Thereby they flatter themselves perhaps that they may do God service; but the Father's love is unknown — never in such a condition can He be fully known. Even when we look at children of God, scattered here and there in the waste, they are trembling and fearful, and practically at a distance, instead of consciously near in peace, as if it were God's will that His children should now stand off in Sinai — distance and terror. Who ever heard even of an earthly father, worthy of the name, so sternly repelling his children? Certainly this is not our Father as we know Him through Christ Jesus. Brethren, it is the spirit of the world which, when sanctioned, invariably tends to destroy the knowledge of the Father, and of our proper relationship, even among His real children, because it necessarily slips more or less into Judaism.

But the Holy Ghost has another work. He convinces the world of the truth they do not know, by the very fact that He is outside the world, and has nothing to do with it. He dwells with the children of God. I do not deny His power in the testimony of the gospel to souls. This is another thing not spoken of here. But, besides, we have His direct immediate action among the disciples. "I have yet many things to say unto you, but ye cannot bear them now. Howbeit when he, the Spirit of truth, is come, he will guide you into all truth." (Verses 12, 13) Thus the disciples, favoured as they were, were far from knowing all that the Lord desired for them, and would have told them if their state had admitted of it. When redemption was accomplished, and Christ was raised from the dead, and the Holy Ghost was given, then they were competent to enter into all the truth, not before. Hence, Christianity awaits not only Christ's coming, but the accomplishment of His work, and also the mission and personal presence of the Holy Ghost, the Comforter, consequent on that work. But He would take no independent place, any more than the Son had. "He shall not speak from himself; but whatever he shall hear, he shall speak: and he will report (or announce) to you things to come. He shall glorify me; for he shall receive of mine, and shall report it to you." (Verses 13, 14)

It is not said, as some think, that He shall not speak about Himself; for the Holy Ghost does speak, and tells us much concerning Himself and His operations; and never so much as under the Christian revelation. The fullest instruction as to the Spirit is in the New Testament; and, pray, who speaks of the Holy Ghost if it be not Himself? Was it merely Paul? or John? or any other man? The fact is, that the Authorised Version gives rather obsolete English. The meaning is, that He shall not speak of His own authority, as if He had nothing to do with the Father and the Son. For He is come here to glorify the Son, just as the Son, when here, was glorifying the Father. And this explains why, although the Holy Ghost is worthy of supreme worship, and of being, equally with the Father and the Son, personally addressed in prayer, yet, having come down for the purpose of animating, directing, and effectuating the work and worship of God's children here, He is never presented in the epistles as directly the object, but rather as the power, of Christian prayer. Therefore, we find them praying in, and never to, the Holy Ghost. At the same time, when we say "God," of course we do mean not only the Father, but the Son, and the Holy Ghost too. In that way, therefore, every intelligent believer knows that he includes the Spirit and the Son with the Father, when he addresses God; because the name "God" does not belong to one person in the

Trinity more than to another. But when we speak of the persons in the Godhead distinctively, and with knowledge of what God has done and is doing, we do well to remind ourselves and one another, that the Spirit has come down and taken a special place among and in the disciples now; the consequence of which is, that He is pleased administratively (without renouncing His personal rights) to direct our hearts thus towards God the Father and the Lord Jesus. He is thus (if we may speak so, as I believe we may and ought reverentially) serving the interests of the Father and the Son here below in the disciples. The fact we have noticed, the administrative position of the Spirit, is thus owing to the work He has voluntarily undertaken for the Father and the Son, though, of course, as a question of His own glory, He is equally to be adored with the Father and the Son, and is always comprehended in God as such.

The rest of the chapter, without entering into minute points, shows that the Lord, about to leave the disciples, would give them a taste of joy — a testimony of what will be. (Verses 16-22) The world might rejoice in having got rid of Him; but He would give His own joy, which would not be taken from them. In measure, this was made good by our Lord's appearing after He rose from the dead; but the full force of it will only be known when He comes again.

Then there is another privilege. The Lord intimates a new character of drawing near to the Father, which they had not yet known. (Verses 23-26) Hitherto they had asked nothing in His name. "In that day," He says, "ye shall ask me nothing." 'We are in "that day" now. "In that day" does not mean in a future day, but in one that is come, instead of using Christ's intervention as Martha proposed, instead of begging Christ to ask[11] the Father,

---

[11] It is remarkable that Martha puts a word (αἰτήσῃ) into Christ's mouth (that is, uses an expression for asking the Father), which is never used nor warranted by Himself. It makes the Lord a mere petitioner, lowering the glory of His person, and obscuring, if not denying, the intimacy of His relationship with the Father.

demanding each thing they needed of Christ Himself, they might reckon on the Father's giving them whatsoever they should ask Him in Christ's name. It is not a question of a Messianic link to get what they wanted, but they would be able to ask the Father in His name themselves. How blessed to know the Father thus hearkening to the children asking in the Son's name! It is of children on earth now the Lord speaks, not of the Father's house by-and-by. Evidently this is a capital truth, bearing powerfully on the nature of the Christian's prayers, as well as on his worship.

It is exactly what accounts for the fact, that we are here on ground quite different from that of the precious and blessed form of prayer which the Lord gave His disciples when they wanted to know how to pray, as John taught his disciples. The Lord necessarily gave them that which was suited to their then condition. Now, I believe, it is little to say that there is not, nor ever was, a formula of prayer comparable with the Lord's prayer. Nor is there, to my thinking, a single petition of that prayer which is not a model for the prayers of His followers ever since; but all remains true and applicable at all times — at least, till our Father's kingdom come. Why, then, was it not employed formally by the apostolic Church? The answer lies in what is now before us. Our Lord here, at the end of His earthly course, informs the disciples that hitherto they had demanded nothing in His name. They had, no doubt, been using the Lord's prayer for some time; nevertheless, they had asked nothing in His name. In that day they were to ask the Father in His name. What I gather from this is, that those who had even used the Lord's prayer, as the disciples had done up to this time, did not know what it was to ask the Father in the Lord's name. They still continued at a comparative distance from their Father; but this is not the Christian state. By the Christian state I mean that in which a man is conscious of his nearness to his God and Father, and able to draw near in virtue of the Holy Ghost even. On the contrary, prayers that suppose a person to be an object of divine displeasure, anxious, and doubtful whether he is to be saved or not — such an experience supposes one incapable of speaking to the Father in Christ's name. It is speaking as still tied and bound with the chain of their sins, instead of standing in known reconciliation, and, with the Spirit of adoption, drawing near to the Father in the name of Christ. Who can honestly, or at least intelligently, deny it? Thus, whatever the blessing through the Lord's ministry, there was certainly an advance here foreshown, founded on redemption, resurrection, and the Spirit given. Why should men limit their thoughts, so as to ignore that incomparable blessing to which even in this gospel Christ was ever pointing, as the fruit of His death and of the presence of the Comforter who would bring in "that day"? It was impossible to furnish a prayer which could reconcile the wants of souls before and after the work of the cross, and the new place consequent on it. And, in fact, the Lord has done the contrary; for He gave the disciples a prayer on principles of everlasting truth, but not anticipating that which His death and resurrection brought to view. Of these new privileges the Holy Ghost sent down was to be the power. Be assured this is no secondary matter, and that traditional views slight unwittingly the infinite efficacy and value of what Christ has wrought, the results of which the Holy Ghost was sent down to apply to our souls. And the gift of that divine person to dwell in us — is this, too, a secondary matter? or is there no radical change which accompanies the work of Christ when accomplished and known? If, indeed, everything be secondary to the supply of man's need, if the unfolding of God's glory and ways in Christ be comparatively a cipher, I understand as much as I hate a principle so base and unbelieving.

It appears to me that the Lord Jesus Himself clearly sets forth the new thing at the highest value, which no general reasonings of men ought to weaken in the least. That immense change, then, let us accept on His authority who cannot deceive us, assured that our brethren, who fail to see how full association with the efficacy of His work and the acceptance of His person, made good in the presence of the Spirit, accounts for the difference between prayer before and prayer after, put no intentional slight on His words in this chapter, or on His work of atonement. But I beseech them to consider whether they are not allowing habits and prejudices to blind them to what seems to me the mind of Christ in this grave question.

In the close of John 16:25-33, the Lord puts, with perfect plainness, both their coming position in His name, and as immediate objects of the Father's affection, and His own place as coming from and going to the Father, above all promise and dispensation. This the disciples thought they saw distinctly; but they were mistaken: their words do not rise higher than — "We believe that thou camest forth from God." The Master thereon warns them of that hour, even then come in spirit, when His rejection should prove their dispersion — deserted, yet not alone, "because the Father is with me." He spoke, that in Him they might have peace, as in the world they should have tribulation. "But be of good cheer: I have overcome the world." It was an enemy of the Father and of them, but an enemy overcome of Him.

On John 17 I must be brief, though its treasures might well invite one to devote ample space to weigh them. A few words, however, may perhaps give the general outline. The Lord, lifting up His eyes to heaven, no longer speaks to the disciples, but turns to His Father. He lays a double ground before Him: one, the glory of His person; the other, the accomplishment of His work. He seeks from the Father for His disciples a place of blessing in association with Himself suitable both to His person and work.

Be it observed, that from verse 6 He develops the relationship of the disciples with His Father, having manifested the Father's name to those who were the Father's, and given them the words which the Father gave Him, and spoken as He did now that they might have His joy fulfilled in them. From verse 14 He develops it with the world, they being not of it, and wholly sanctified from it, while sent into it like Himself. And observe, here, that He has given them the Father's word (λόγον) for their testimony (as before His words, ῥήματα), but sanctifies them, not by this only, which kept them from the evil of the world, but by Himself, always separate from sin, but now made higher than the heavens, so as to fill them with an object there that could engage and expand and purify their affections. From verse 20 He extends this place of privilege and responsibility to those who should believe on Him through the word of the apostles, the moral unity of verse 11 being now enlarged into a unity of testimony, that the world might believe that the Father sent the Son; and carried onward, even to the display of glory — "I in them, and thou in me" — when they shall be perfected into one, and the world shall know (not then "believe") that the Father sent the Son, and loved them as He loved Him. (Compare 2 Thess. 1:10)

Lastly, from verse 24 to the end, we have, if possible, deeper things than even these; and here the Lord expresses His heart's desire, for it is no longer, as before, in the form of a request (ἐρωτῶ) but, "Father, I will," or desire (θέλω). This word indicates a new character of plea: "I desire that they also, whom thou hast given me, be with me where I am." The earlier section laid His person and His work as the ground for His being glorified on high, according to the title of the one, and in the accomplishment of the other. Verse 24, as it were, takes up that position of glory with the Father before the world was, into which Christ has gone, with His heart's expression of desire that they should be with Him where He is, that they might behold His glory, which the Father gave Him; "for thou lovedst me before the foundation of the world." Thus, if the central portion gave us the disciples on the earth in relation with the Father on the one hand, and in total separation from the world on the other, with subsequent believers brought into one, both in testimony and in glory by-and-by before the world, the closing verses take up Christians, as it were, with the Father in an unearthly, heavenly glory, and His desire that they should be with Him there. It is not merely sought for them, that they should be thoroughly, as far as, could be, in His own place of relationship with the Father, and apart from the world, but also that they should be brought into intimacy of nearness with Himself before the Father. Then, in verse 25, the breach between the world and the Father and the Son being complete, He says, "O righteous Father, the world hath not known thee; but I have known thee, and these have known that thou hast sent me." There is always this opposition between the Father and the world, proved by His person in the world. But the disciples had known that the Father sent the Son, as the Son knew the Father. He had made known to them the Father's name, and would yet more, "that the love wherewith thou hast loved me may be in them, and I in them;" this last verse bringing into them, as it were, the Father's love, as the Son knew it, which was the secret source of all the blessing and glory, and Christ Himself in them, whose life by the Spirit was the sole nature capable of enjoying all. Thus they should have a present enjoyment of the Father, and of Christ, according to the place of nearness they had as thus associated with Him.

On the concluding chapters of our gospel I cannot speak particularly now. Yet I must, in passing point out that even in these solemn closing scenes the glory of the Son's person is ever the prominent figure. Hence we have no notice of His agony in the garden, nor of God's forsaking Him on the tree. Matthew depicts Him as the suffering Messiah, according to psalms and prophets; Mark, as the rejected Servant and Prophet of God; Luke, as the perfect and obedient Son of man, who shrank from no trial either for soul or body, but even on the cross prayed for His enemies, filling a poor sinner's heart with the good news of salvation, and committing His spirit with unwavering confidence to His Father. The point here is the Son of God with the world, the Jews especially being His enemies. Hence, John tells us (John 18) what no other gospel does, that when the band came to take Jesus, led by one who knew too well the spot where His heart had so often, poured itself out to the Father, at once they went backward, and fell to the ground. Do you suppose Matthew let it slip? or that Mark and Luke never heard of it? Is it conceivable that a fact so notorious — the very world being the objects of the divine power that cast them prostrate to the ground — could be hidden from, or forgotten by, friends or foes? Or if even men (not to speak of the Spirit's power) would forget such a thing, did the rest think it too slight for their mention? All such suppositions are preposterous. The true explanation is, that the gospels are written with divine design, and that here, as everywhere, John records a fact which falls in with the Spirit's object in his gospel. Did these men come to seize Jesus? He was going to be a prisoner, and to die; in the one case, as much as in the other, He would prove it was not of man's constraint, but of His own will and in obedience to His Father's. He was a willing prisoner, and a willing victim. If none could take His life unless He laid it down, so none could take Him prisoner unless He gave Himself up. Nor was it simply that He could ask His Father for twelve legions of angels, as He says in Matthew; but, in John, did He want angels? They might and did ascend and descend on Him as Son of man; but He had only to speak, and it was done. He is God.

The moment He said, "I am he," without lifting a finger, or even audibly expressing a desire, they fell to the ground. Could this scene be suitably given by any other than John? Could he leave it out who presents his Master as the Son and the Word who was God?

Again, we have our Lord's calm rebuke to Peter, who had cut off the ear of Malchus. Let Luke alone tell us of the Lord's gracious healing (for Jehovah's power to heal was not absent); John alone adds, "The cup which my Father hath given me, shall I not drink it?" He preserves throughout His personal dignity and His conscious relationship, but withal in perfect submission to His Father.

Then follows the notice of Peter's sad history with that other disciple which was known to the high priest. Next, our Lord is before the high priest, Caiaphas, as previously before his father-in-law Annas, and, finally, before Pilate. Suffice it to say, that the one point which meets us here, as distinct from the other gospels, is His person. Not that He was not King of the Jews, but His kingdom is not of this world, not from hence, and He Himself is born and come into the world to bear witness to the truth. Here it is the Jews insist He ought by their law to die, because He made Himself the Son of God. (John 19) Here, too, He answers Pilate, after scourging and mockery, "Thou couldest have no power at all against me, except it were given thee from above: therefore he that delivered me unto thee hath the greater sin." (Verse 11) It was the Jews, led on by Judas, that had this greater sin. The Jew ought to have known better than Pilate, and Judas better than the Jew. The glory of the Son was too bright for their eyes. Afterwards there is another characteristic scene, the blending of the most perfect human affection with His divine glory — He confides His mother to the disciple whom He loved. (Verses 25-27)

The gospel which most of all shows Him to be God is careful to prove Him man. The Word was made flesh.

"After this, Jesus knowing that all things were now accomplished, that the scripture might be fulfilled, saith, I thirst." I know not a more sweet and wonderful proof of how completely He was divinely superior to all circumstances. He had before Him with perfect distinctness all the truth of God. Here was a scripture which He remembers as unaccomplished. It was a word in Psalm 69. It was enough. "I thirst." What absorption in His Father's will! "Now there was set a vessel full of vinegar: and they filled a spunge with vinegar, and put it upon hyssop, and put it to his mouth. When Jesus therefore had received the vinegar, he said, It is finished." (Verses 29, 30) Where could such a word as this be but in John? Who could say, "It is finished," except Jesus in John? Matthew and Mark both give our Lord saying, "My God, my God, why hast thou forsaken me?" This could not be in John. Luke gives us, "Father, into thy hands I commend my spirit," because there the perfect man never abandons His perfect reliance on God. God must, in the judgment of our sins, forsake Him, but He would never forsake God. The atonement would not have been what it is unless God had thus forsaken Him. But in Luke it is the sign of absolute trust in His Father, and not God's abandonment. In John He says, "It is finished," because He is the Son, by whom all worlds were made, Who but He could say it? Who but John could mention that He delivered up (παρέδωκε) His spirit? In every point of difference the fullest possible proof of divine glory and wisdom appears in these gospels. Put to death no doubt He was but at the same time it was His own voluntary will; and who could have this about death itself but a divine person? In a mere man it would be sin; in Him it was perfection. Then come the soldiers, breaking the legs of the others crucified with Him; but finding Jesus dead already, one pierces His side, land forthwith came thereout blood and water. And he that saw it bare record."

Thus a double scripture is fulfilled. The apostle John does not quote many scriptures; but when he does, the person of the Son is the great point. Accordingly this was the case now; for not a bone was to be broken. It was true. Nevertheless, He was to be pierced. He was singled out from the others, even while dead between the dying thieves. He has a place even here that belonged to Him alone.

Joseph charges himself with the body too; and Nicodemus, who came first by night is here by day, honoured by association with Jesus crucified, of whom he had been ashamed once, spite of the miracles He was doing.

In John 20 is the resurrection, and this in a remarkable light. No such outward circumstance is here as in Matthew, no soldiers trembling, no walk with disciples, but as ever the person of God's Son, though disciples prove how little they entered into the truth. Peter "saw, and believed. For as yet they knew not the Scriptures, that He must rise again from the dead." (Verses 8, 9) It was evidence; and there is no moral value in accepting on evidence. Believing the word of God has moral value, because it gives God credit for truth. A man gives up himself to confide in

God. Believing the Scriptures, therefore, has another character altogether from a judgment formed on a matter of fact. Mary Magdalene, with as little understanding of the Scriptures as they, stood without at the sepulchre weeping, when they went to their own homes. Jesus meets her in her sorrow, dries her tears, and sends her to the disciples with a message of His resurrection. But He does not permit her to touch Him. In Matthew the other women even retain Him by the feet. Why? The reason appears to be that in the earlier gospel it is the pledge of a bodily presence for the Jews in the latter day; for whatever be the consequences of Jewish unbelief now, God is faithful. The gospel of John has here no purpose of showing God's promises for the circumcision; but, on the contrary, sedulously detaches the disciples from Jewish thoughts. Mary Magdalene is a sample or type of this. The heart must be taken off His bodily presence. "Touch me not; for I am not yet ascended to my Father." The Christian owns Christ in heaven. As the apostle says, even if we had known Christ after the flesh, "henceforth know we him no more." The cross, as we know it, closes all connection with even Him in this world. It is the same Christ manifested in life here upon earth. John shows us, in Mary Magdalene contrasted with the woman of Galilee, the difference between the Christian and the Jew. It is not outward corporeal presence on earth, but a greater nearness, though He is ascended to heaven, because of the power of the Holy Ghost. "But go to my brethren, and say unto them, I ascend unto my Father, and your Father; and to my God, and your God." (Verse 17) Never had He put Himself and His disciples so together before.

The next scene (verses 19-23) is the disciples gathered together. It is not a message individually, but they are assembled on the same first day at evening, and Jesus stands, spite of closed doors, in the midst of them, and showed them His hands and His side. "Then said Jesus to them again, Peace be unto you: as my Father hath sent me, even so send I you. And when he had said this, he breathed on them, and saith unto them, receive ye the Holy Ghost: whose soever sins ye remit, they are remitted unto them;

and whose soever sins ye retain, they are retained." It is a picture of the assembly that was about to be formed at Pentecost — and this is the assembly's function. They have authority from God to retain or to remit sins — not at all as a question of eternal forgiveness, but administratively or in discipline. For instance, when a soul is received from the world, what is this but remitting sins? The Church again, by restoring a soul put outside, puts its seal, as it were, to the truth of what God has done, acts upon it, and thus remits the sin. On the other hand, supposing a person is refused fellowship, or is put away after being received, there is the retaining of sins. There is no real difficulty, if men did not pervert Scripture into a means of self-exaltation, or cast away truth, on the other side, revolting from the frightful misuse known in popery. But Protestants have failed to keep up consciously the possession of so great a privilege, founded on the presence of the Holy Ghost.

Eight days after we have another scene. (Verses 24-29) One of the disciples, Thomas, had not been with the others when Jesus had thus appeared. Clearly there is a special teaching in this. Seven days had run their course before Thomas was with the disciples, when the Lord Jesus Christ meets his unbelief, pronouncing those more blessed who saw not, and yet believed. Of what is this the symbol? Of Christian faith? The very contrary. Christian faith is essentially believing on Him that we have not seen: believing, "we walk by faith, not by sight." But the day is coming when there will be the knowledge and the sight of glory in the earth. So the millennium will differ from what is now. I deny not that there will be faith, as there was faith required when Messiah was on earth. Then faith saw underneath the veil of flesh this deeper glory. But, evidently, proper Christianity is after redemption was wrought, and Christ takes His place on high, and the Holy Ghost is sent down, when there is nothing but faith. Thomas, then, represents the slow mind of unbelieving Israel, seeing the Lord after the present cycle of time is completely over. What makes it the more remarkable is the contrast with Mary Magdalene in the previous verses, who is the type of the Christian taken out of Judaism, and no longer admitted to Jewish contact with the Messiah, but witnesses of Him in ascension.

Mark, too, the confession of Thomas; not a word about "My Father and your Father," but, "My Lord, and my God." Just so the Jew will acknowledge Jesus. They shall look on Him whom they pierced, and own Jesus of Nazareth to be their Lord and their God. (See Zechariah 12) It is not association with Christ, and He not ashamed to call us brethren, according to the position He has taken as man before His and our God and Father, but the recognition forced on Him by the marks of the cross, which drew out the confession of Christ's divine glory and Lordship.

In John 21, the appended scene is the fishing. After a night of failure, a vast multitude of fish is taken in the net, without breaking it or risking the ships (Luke 5), or the need of gathering the good into vessels and of casting the bad away. (Matt. 13) This I conceive to be a gathering in from the Gentiles. The sea is continually used in contrast to the land in prophetic Scripture. Thus, if the last was the Jewish scene when the Church state closed, this is the figure of the Gentiles in the great day of the earth's jubilee, the age to come contrasted with this age. From verse 15 to the end is the deep personal dealing of our Lord with Peter; also John's place. As I have no doubt there is a significance typically in what we have just glanced at, so it appears to me with regard to this also. The intermediate ministry of Paul is, of course, not here noticed; for he was the witness of Christ glorified in heaven — Head of the Church His body, wherein is neither Jew nor Gentile. To Peter, the Lord, thoroughly restoring his soul after proving him to the core, commits His sheep and lambs (His Jewish flock, as we know from elsewhere). A violent end comes, though to God's glory. But if the full heavenly testimony is left for its own due place in Paul's completing the word of God — that hidden mystery, John is seen witnessing in principle to the end. (Compare verses 22, 23 with the Revelation) However, I do not enlarge here, but rather apologise for the time that I have occupied in going over so large an extent of God's word. I pray the Lord that even these suggestions may be blessed of God in stirring up fresh desire to study, and weigh, and pray over these precious gospels. Surely it will be sweet reward now, if God deign thereby to give some of His children to approach His word with more reverence and a more childlike trust in every word He has written. May He vouchsafe this through Christ our Lord.

Printed in Great Britain
by Amazon